# INTUITION:
# LANGUAGE OF THE SOUL

BOOK ONE

Tyger Kahn

BookBaby
Portland, Oregon

Tyger Kahn/BookBaby Publishing
13909 NE Airport Way
Portland, Oregon 97230
www.BookBaby.com

Cover Illustration © 2016 Mordechai Edel

Book Layout © 2016 BookDesignTemplates.com

For speaking engagements, consulting services, or information
about bulk purchases, visit TygerKahn.com or contact her via
www.tygerassistant.com

For more on the cover artist: www.EdelArtist.com

Intuition: Language of the Soul/Tyger Kahn. -- 1st ed.
ISBN (Print) 978-1-48357-252-9
ISBN (Ebook) 978-1-48357-253-6

*To my father, Yechezkal HaCohen ben Chana, who kept the flame of our lineage alight my whole life. This is my gift to you.*
*Aunt Friday bat Chana, may her name be a blessing; Raphael Simcha Dovid ben Aharon HaCohen, z''l.*
*Rabbi Berry and Nechama Farkash, Rabbi Mordechai and Rochie Farkash*
*To my twin sister Tobina, Monique, Lilly, Zoe, Debahlah, Erin, Johnna, Sarale, Nicole, Maia Tamar*
*To my brother Ari Todd, Eliyahu, T.R.*
*To Kalmen the Math Magician*
*To the Docs: Adam Rinde, Bob Wolhman, Martin Herman, Yasuhiro Matsumura, Kathy Moorhead, Kathy Erickson, Tom Sweeny, Nasi, and Shirley*
*Lastly, Joseph, my rock: Warriors and eternal friends— my love and gratitude for the journey.*
*You are all my family.*

"Tyger Kahn has written a wonderful book that the world needs to read. Her soul-filling anecdotes leave you with both questions and answers."

Troy Carter
Founder and CEO, Atom Factory

# TABLE OF CONTENTS

# INTUITION:
# LANGUAGE OF THE SOUL

BOOK ONE

# From Tibet to Sinai

Our future is not set in stone; we have more than one. My journey as a clairvoyant took me to dimensions both worldly and otherwise. The most important lesson being: make Heaven your partner.

*On the night I left this world, I dreamt that I was walking with people of different ages and races. We descended down a circular path in silence. Suddenly, we began an ascent towards a ceiling of indigo lightening. I could see many levels with gates. Once I reached my "floor" I walked into a space where I perceived people as forms of light, communicating telepathically with one another through colored rays projected from their hearts. And though it was a place of bliss, I was miserable and wanted to leave. I missed my twin sister. I knew these "people" were no longer alive and I did not want to ruin the pure atmosphere with my negative energy, so I looked for a place to hide, clutching my knees to my chest and praying with all my might. A beautiful woman about seven feet tall appeared and scooped me up in her arms. She kissed my forehead and . . . moments later, I woke up in my bed.*

*I told my boyfriend at the time that I had died but was sent back. I described the place in detail and then I repeated the words I had heard while I was there, whispering them over and over like a mantra:* Ribbono shel Olam (*Master of the Universe*).

*Two days later, I was in the emergency room at Overlake Hospital, where they discovered I had lost two-thirds of my body's blood. I was literally dying. My hematocrit (the volume percentage of red blood cells in the blood) was 13 percent (the normal level for a woman ranges from 38 to 45 percent). The emergency medical team that worked on me shook their heads in disbelief at my chart and blood pressure count. The technician at the hospital had never seen a conscious person with a number that low. The doctors gave me only hours to live.*

*Later, during my recovery, doctors rationalized that my body must have learned to adjust with little oxygen, akin to a mountain climber in the Himalayas. Well, that is one way of looking at a miracle! (Which two oncologists said I was.) One thing for sure: I was not going to go back to the way things were before.*

*Shortly after midnight on Friday, November 21, 2008, I removed the amulet on my neck, a gift from my former guru, and held my arm out to receive a blood transfusion that lasted until eight o'clock the next morning. Believe it or not, while this was going on, I requested for and ate an entire chicken. No small act, considering I had been a vegetarian for ten years. But I was determined to make it, and I figured the meat would give me strength.*

*Then I recalled a prayer I had heard my father say when I was a child:* Ani Ma'amin, *which was sung by Jews in the cattle cars on the way to the concentration camps. It means* I believe redemption will come, *and I felt these words in my Soul. As the words came out of my lips and the blood went into my veins, I felt myself returning to the world—and I remembered the message from the other side:* We are never alone, we are loved, and heaven has a better plan for us then we see ourselves.

*Even if we are clairvoyant.*

You have a body and a soul, which have completely different natures, a duality that needs to be integrated in order to fulfill your purpose in life. Before incarnating into your body, your soul made a vow to be holy.

Still . . .

Most of us stumble through life, stuck in patterns. By continuing on the course we set for ourselves long ago, determining the future is more of connect-the-dots. When we are headed in a direction that will seriously hinder our destiny, the Creator will set circumstances in motion to help align us back to our path. Sometimes these events are shattering and painful. We think we are being punished, and it is impossible to see any good in the experience. It may take years—or lifetimes—before the gifts from such events are revealed. However, there will come a time when the picture will be clear. A certain portion of our destiny is preordained—parents, particular gifts, and encounters with others—that will either assist or hinder us in fulfilling our purpose. Fortunately, since we have been given free will, referred to as *bechira* in Hebrew, we also choose the path we walk on, and these choices set realities into motion that contain both the DNA of our soul's mission and the keys to carry it though.

But what path do you walk? How do you choose?

Start by recognizing that you have a spark of the Creator within you. It is the soul's Divine inheritance to connect straight to this infinite Source. But where and how do we begin?

Our body is the vehicle with which our soul interacts with the world. The longer the soul stays in the physical body, the more it forgets its vow of holiness, until all that is known is the pull of this world. This amnesia can last a lifetime, or only temporarily block your soul from its true purpose. It depends on how much the soul is introduced to meaning doing it's time on earth. That is the aim of this book; to remind your soul what it knows is true.

Think of your fingers. How much significance do you attribute to these digits? Fingers can help bring a new life into this world, plant food, communicate, show love, and create beauty. Because they hold such great potential in creation, so too is their effect on destruction. It is the finger that pulls the trigger and destroys a world. Imagine the rest of your body and what extraordinary effects it can have on reality.

The finger is the opening to understanding your soul. When you understand what your finger can do, you can begin to realize the full impact of your presence here, which is temporary.

Our actions during our lifetime translate into the clothing the soul will wear in the world to come. I know because I have seen these garments of Light. Having left this world for a brief time, I can affirm that the soul lives on.

## A Note about This Book

The word *soul* generally refers to the spiritual part of a person's being. This book explains how there is a feminine aspect *(neshama) of a* being's spirit, as well as an instinctive, male aspect *(nefesh)*, which I often describe as the "animal" soul. As I discuss this duality in chapter

1, you will notice *soul* often refers to the feminine, spiritual soul, individually. At times, it may also refer to either the feminine *or* the masculine aspects as complementary but—for the sake of discussion—separate souls, *or* it may refer to both male and female aspects integrated together as a single unit. This is deliberate, and the intended meaning should be clear from the context. Another detail to keep in mind: in my writing you will see many references to Jewish tradition, such as the practice of not spelling the name of G-d or alluding to Him with various other names.

I am descended from an ancient mystical lineage, traced back to the original high priest, Aharon, as well as King David. Nevertheless, many years passed before I fully understood the significance and obligations of such ancestry, and what it could teach me on how to live. First, I had to embark on a spiritual journey from Tibet to Sinai. My odyssey led me to train with Tibetan monks and a Grand Master healer, traversing the maze of psychic phenomena. All the while, I was ignoring my body and material needs.

Only when I reached the spiritual highs and realized I had no physical way to live, that my body was dying, could I escape the quicksand. I grabbed a hold of the strings of my ancestors, realizing the lessons they had to offer. In doing so, I could finally begin to heal.

CHAPTER ONE

# Reconciling Your Spiritual and Animal Souls

*I was driving with my loved one when I saw, through my window, a monkey in a building where animals were kept. We stopped in front of the building and I went inside. Many creatures of strange sizes and looks rushed to greet me. I sat down to play with them, when suddenly a large owl began biting me. When I asked it to stop, the owl turned into a beast with ginger fur, orange as flames, angry that he was kept in a cell while his brother, Man, roamed free . . .*

## Main Misconceptions

I often come across two common misconceptions:

*We are separate from G-d.*
*We must sacrifice the desires of the body in order to be spiritual.*

Regarding the first misconception, my response is simple: how can we be separate from that which we derive? Is a cell separate from other cells—from the living organism of which it is a part? Is a star separate from a galaxy—within galaxy, within universe? What happens when a cell thinks it is independent from other cells? When it disregards its connection and goes rogue? It begins to function abnormally, becoming diseased and eventually destroying itself and the vehicle it feeds off. I liken this to the ego that believes it exists independently.

**Divinity is within; we are never separate from our Creator.**

Numerous individuals have overcome unbelievable hardships under the toughest conditions. When you speak with these impressive Souls or hear the interviews, the unifying thread is the strength of their faith and connection to the Divine.

Regarding the second misconception: the erroneous belief that in order to be spiritual, one has to sacrifice the needs of the body. Not only is it impractical to ignore one aspect of ourselves, it even denies the reality of our existence.

We have come to this world to balance and build our spiritual essence along with our physical bodies. There is no shortcut to achieving this balance if we are to function sustainably. Our lower and higher natures contain intense yearnings of opposing forces, creating a life-long internal struggle. The spiritual soul does not desire food or pleasure, but without these things our physical bodies cannot go on living. Likewise, without the spiritual soul, the animal soul finds no peace, no purpose to life. We all have a little bit of a beast within us, which becomes a problem when we do not exercise it through the right channels. We have a body that has inherent desires and needs. Our essence and purpose in life is to integrate our instinctive nature with our intrinsic holiness.

## The Struggle

According to the Tanya, the core document in the study of Hassidic and Kabbalistic thought and a practical guide for living in service of the Almighty, this is the "life-long struggle between two cities." These 'cities' represent the two souls that live within us: the animal soul that on its own will always choose what feels pleasurable, even when it is poisonous, and our spirit, which only desires to go back to the Light.

This duality also corresponds to raw and refined energy, with raw energy correlating with the animal soul and refined energy correlating with the Divine soul. Uniting these opposing natures only takes place here, in this world. When we die, the conflict is over: they separate and return to their place of origin—the body to the earth, and the spirit to a dimension we know as Heaven.

Intuition creates a bridge between raw and refined energy, allowing your soul's duality to integrate. The physical aspect often receives more attention and energy (and rewarded by society for doing so). However, when the body commits an action that conflicts with its divine nature, our soul weeps. Though most of us cannot hear, we feel the pain in varying degrees. When you access your intuition, it enables you to direct your instinctive nature, to align its actions with the requirements of your spirit. Believe me, whether you realize it consciously or not, every individual inherently knows the needs of their soul.

One night my boyfriend appeared to me in a dream, encapsulated within a silver energy field, or aura. He told me, "I am the soul of X. You will recognize me through this body that clothes me. Please, tell this body that its actions are causing me to grieve." Then he told me in detail what, exactly, his body was up to when I was not around.

I woke up, looked at my partner (we will call him 'X') asleep in our bed and thought, "Nah . . . just a nightmare," and fell back asleep. Once again, my X's spirit appeared before me, this time pleading I speak with his body, which was deaf to his cries. When morning came and I told my partner about my dream, you would not have needed to be psychic to know that he was shocked. He confessed immediately.

Years later, when I studied the Tanya Chassidic *Kabbalah* (Jewish mysticism) and I reached where it speaks of being born with two souls that are polar opposites of each other, I did not need convincing.

**Understanding the Animal: Betrayal**
Until every individual has elevated and channeled his or her animal instincts to more conscious choices, at some point we will experience betrayal or, worse, betray someone else. And the arrow usually comes from or goes to those we care about the most: our core primary relationships, the ones that hit us right in the heart. So what can we do? How do we protect ourselves or at least soothe the sting of the pain?

Let us take a look at the life of King David, primary author of the book of *Tehillim*, the Psalms, for a remedy. Before David becomes king he is bitterly betrayed by King Saul, his mentor and father-in-law. Hunted and scorned by Saul's armies, vilified unjustly, David has to go into hiding. After battles upon battles, he finally becomes king himself, only to be betrayed by his beloved son, Absalom, who raises an army to kill his king and father. After surviving the heartbreak, including the death of his first son, King David goes home. Shortly after, he sees the beautiful Bathsheba on a roof-top. Incensed with desire, he boldly sends her husband, Uzziah, to the front lines of a heavy battle, knowing it is unlikely he will survive. True to his scheme, Uzziah dies. King David, filled with remorse and in the midst of despair, reaches into his soul—not as a King but as a simple man—and is granted grace. He eventually writes the Psalms from both sorrow and joy. In doing so, he purifies, uplifts, and displays gratitude regarding the miracle and sanctity of life. King David was a great prophet who knew that in the future, humanity would still be struggling with the same core issues of his own time.

The Psalms are keys to opening gates of higher consciousness. Consistently using psalms as a source of prayer helps to refine and direct our instinctual nature, elevating our choices. In turn, this will allow our higher soul to communicate more effectively with our animal soul—with the will of our emotion and physical being. Have you ever ate too much junk food, watched too much TV, or simply made some serious mistakes? In life, it is very easy to become saturated with too much junk. Junk food, junk television, junk Internet. The Psalms are the remote that helps us to switch to a better station.

So, whether you betrayed someone or have been betrayed by others, do not give up hope. Transformative redemption is possible—we just have to ask for it, and the effects can last through the ages. The second son of King David and Bathsheba, Solomon, grew to become King Solomon, considered the wisest individual to ever live. The legendary King Solomon rebuilt the Holy Temple and restored glory to Israel.

## Tyger Teaching: Soothe Your Soul with Psalms

King David wrote the Psalms for all generations to purify, transmute, and redeem themselves. Regardless of your religious or spiritual identity, these prayers were designed to help you unite the two aspects of your soul. This is especially true when you are undergoing hardship. Prayer transforms us internally, which will create the change you wish to see. For at least forty days, every morning say one Psalm that speaks to your spirit. Here is one of my favorite examples:

### Psalm 91: for Protection

*O thou that dwellest in the secret place of the Most High*

*will abide under the shadow of the Almighty.*

*I will say of the Lord, "He is my refuge and my fortress,*

*my G-d, in whom will I trust."*

*Surely he will deliver thee*

*from the snare of the fowler*

*and from the destructive pestilence.*

*He shall cover thee with his feathers,*

*and under his wings shall thou trust;*

*his truth shall be thy shield and buckler*

*Thou shall not be afraid of the terror by night,*

*Nor for the arrow that flieth by day,*

*Nor for the pestilence that walketh in the darkness,*

*nor for the destruction that wasteth at noonday.*

*A thousand shall fall at thy side,*

*and ten thousand at thy right hand,*

*but it shall not come nigh thee*

*Only with thine eyes shalt thou behold the reward of the wicked*
*Because thou has made the Lord who is my refuge,*
*even the Most High, thy habitation,*
*There shall no evil befall thee*
*Neither shall any plague come neigh thy dwelling*
*For he shall give his angels charge over thee to keep thee in all ways*
*They shall bear thee up in their hands,*
*lest thou dash thy foot against a stone.*
*Thou shall tread upon the lion and adder;*
*The young lion and the asp shalt thou trample underfoot.*
*Because he hath set his love upon me therefore will I deliver him*
*I will set him on high because he hath known my name*
*He shall call upon me, and I will answer him;*
*I will be with him in trouble,*
*I will deliver him and honor him.*
*With long life I will satisfy him*
*and show him my salvation.*

Other helpful options:
- Psalm 15 for mental clarity
- Psalm 20 for acute situations
- Psalm 25 for forgiveness
- Psalm 28 for loneliness
- Psalm 49 for anger
- Psalm 100 for gratitude
- Psalm 147 for the broken hearted

## Bridging Spirit and Matter

Imagine fraternal twins before they are born, occupying one womb, much like the dualities of the two souls living within a person. In Genesis, we learn the story of a set of twins: Esau and Jacob. Esau was a hunter with a passionate nature, prone to violence and war for the ego's sake. Jacob, his twin brother, was a gentle shepherd who aspired to connect with his soul. A whole journey takes place between the brothers of fighting and turmoil, much like our inner battle between our physical and spiritual desires, which keep vying for power. Despite this conflict, the brothers overcome their differences for a period and share in a short redemption through acceptance and forgiveness. This story illustrates the possibilities of humanity: if twins like Esau and Jacob—polar opposites—can accept their differences and make peace, at least for a moment, there is hope we can do the same within ourselves. This is especially true as we become more familiar with our intuitive nature, the language of our higher soul.

Kabbalah teaches us that there is a link between the spiritual and material worlds. There should be no area in either nature or in human life from which the Omnipotent is excluded.

### Refining, Not Denying, Our Instincts

Have you ever been in a situation where you were about to do something that made you feel uneasy? Maybe you went ahead with it because you felt pressured by others, or because you wanted to be accepted (read: "loved"). Then, even after the situation unfolded, you did not feel right…

Perhaps nothing dramatic happened, but the choice you made forced you to compromise. Faced with cognitive dissonance from your actions not matching your values, you now had to rationalize your actions. Then, the struggle to live with truth and dignity becomes harder and harder. Even if no one else notices, you begin to hurt inside from the guilt and the doubt—but not enough to make you stop doing whatever is creating that pain. So, you keep doing the same thing, until one day you look in the mirror and your eyes have a hard, cold, glare that you never saw before.

That initial feeling of uneasiness was your soul crying, but you could not hear it. This is not unusual; after all, how could you hear it? Your spirit is buried under a mountain of trauma and pain from years of neglect. When we fail to refine our instincts, the will of the animal soul will dominate the needs of the higher soul. This is why many religions try to squash the desires of the body. But that does not work! When someone tries to contain us, our animal fights even harder for what it wants, unless we change and refine our internal and external patterns.

Alternatively, when we refrain from doing something without truly understanding why, it is like being on a diet. In a moment of weakness, we will act out and justify our moral blindness—literally unable to see how those actions are harmful. This continues until...BOOM! We finally see the effects of our actions. We have all been there—who has not felt ashamed and disappointed with their actions at some point?

Our souls came into this world to experience and create meaning through our physicality. The ultimate goal: *for the body to act from the will of the soul, not the other way around.*

Remember, the goal is not to deny or rid ourselves of the animal within. We are human beings having a human experience. Of course we need our instincts or we would lose the will to survive! Our spiritual soul, without its animal nature to vivify or animate the body, will depart it.

### Lost on a Mountain

When I trained in the meditation school, "we are not the body, we are the soul," was the fundamental teaching, a mantra we repeated in classes and retreats.

It is a truth, but only half of it.

After a few months of chanting, I noticed a significant number of students facing physical and financial trouble. Why?

Consider this; have you ever been on a fast (or even just really hungry)? What did you find yourself thinking about most? Something spiritual...or when and what you were going to eat? Perhaps you felt lighter—maybe even high. I guarantee that you were pondering your stomach's needs before those of your spiritual soul—and that is perfectly natural! The point is to be aware of your spiritual soul in everything you do in life. This will elevate your needs to a different level, rather than repress them. The goal is to learn to elevate and direct our instinctual nature to a higher purpose.

For example, meaningless sex. It may satisfy your animal soul, but it will never make you feel fulfilled. You are ignoring the spiritual soul's desire. A committed relationship is more fulfilling because we take the next step, to marriage and inclusion of the Creator. In deepest Kabbalah, two people entwined as one are as close to divinity as possible in this world. The sexual act can create a new being—one of the most powerful energies in the world. Therefore, like nuclear fusion, it should be respected and used wisely.

Other examples of balancing the animal with the spiritual: listening to beautiful music rather than caustic sounds, using your mouth for kindness instead of slander. Everywhere your body goes, so does your soul.

We are born with particular gifts and talents, as well as the destructive force that prevents them. For instance, what other mammal destroys its nest? Yet we continue to ignore the data on the decline of our environment. Further, living in today's world has made our instincts go on overdrive, aligning us to energies of fear. When we are frightened, unhappy, or depressed, our intuition is blocked—and we need intuition to live in a conscious manner (more on this later). Individually or collectively, when we ignore our inner voices, society breaks down.

Intuition often does not make sense; it does not correlate to left-brain activities such as rational thinking and logic. It takes a very refined body to know what is right for the soul because an intuitive message will often not feel pleasurable to our animal desires. How many of us like to alter our patterns? Especially when we have unconsciously managed to operate for years like this. Becoming conscious can be painful. It forces us to take responsibility for our actions, which might not feel good.     Ancient Jewish sages tell us that two angels walk by our sides throughout life, recording our actions. In the world to come, our deeds will be judged by both prosecutor and defender. We are tested until we break through the chains that bind us. Even when it appears that we are winning the battle to integrate our dual natures, we learn again that it is a life-long struggle. As described by the Spanish philosopher Maimonides, "One should see the world, and see himself as a scale with an equal balance of good and evil. When he does one good deed, the scale is tipped to the good—he and the world are saved. When he does one evil deed, the scale is tipped to the bad—he and the world are destroyed."

Our future, individually and collectively, lies in balancing good and evil with our hands and mouths. Our actions and words are what make the difference.

**Tying it All Together**
In my life, I followed the path of spirituality where it led, trying to grab hold of the flow for myself. It led me to ashrams and meditation schools as I tried to learn to integrate my psychic abilities with my life. After all that I have gone through, I want to give the tools that I have found to be most beneficial to not only my growth, what I believe would be most helpful for anyone to learn.

I am a clairvoyant. For those of you that are not clairvoyants, this may seem like a far removed idea; something you will never grasp, let alone do yourselves. However, there is a sixth sense called intuition that we all have. Don't worry; I will delve into it later. Yes, we might not all be clairvoyant, but everyone is intuitive.

If I am going to do anything with this book, I hope to impart on you the fundamentals in how to train yourselves in a safe way to open your intuition. There are many paths to doing this that can harm your soul and your being irreparably. I want you all to come away healthier. The way I have found to do so is through Kabbalah. You might have heard of it lately in the media as some form of 'mysticism' popular among celebrities, but don't be so quick to judge! Kabbalah contains some very powerful ideas and can help you remain rooted to this world by understanding how the body and soul thrive when they work in tandem.

This is not just a spiritual world; we don't escape our body. It is imperative to learn how to use it effectively, in a way that will help us rather than hinder us. When you ignore your body, it can lead to chaos. Kabbalah offers rhythm, roundedness, stability, and consistency. It will help you center yourself amidst the world of fad-culture that we live in, which jumps from one extreme to the next. These ancient remedies, which still hold true today, work in synergy with your physical, mental, spiritual, and emotional selves. Of course, we are all a work in progress. Do not expect complete balance and perfection; it is a lifelong process.

This book will focus heavily on my personal knowledge of the world of the unseen: auras and their patterns, energy, clairvoyance, dream interpretations, and much more. As I reveal my knowledge of this world, I must also introduce Jewish mystical remedies for the body and soul. Why? Most people can live a full, happy life without delving into the world of the unseen. Therefore, to breach this subject is tricky and can even be dangerous. It is imperative to center yourself when learning about higher spiritual concepts. This will ensure that you remain grounded and healthy in your search for spirituality. Jewish mysticism, called *Kabbalah*, is the most effective body of knowledge that I have found to do this. Kabbalah provides basic remedies for balancing and integrating the body and soul. These ancient practices can help to open gates of awareness and understanding on our quest for self-discovery.

One of the biggest challenges we face on a journey of self-discovery is going to extremes. What does this mean? We ignore parts of ourselves to the point of self-destruction. This can be true on both sides of the spectrum, physically and energetically. These concepts relate to every aspect of existence and will therefore be addressed throughout the book. Life is about finding a medium (not a psychic medium!).

CHAPTER TWO

# Reading Energy

*A woman about to give birth flew above me on a ladder. The boy dropped in her uterus, ready to descend to the world, when a fully developed arm with the strength of an army reached down from her womb and pulled me up with them . . .*

## Seeing and Hearing the Future

A clairvoyant, also known as a psychic, is an individual who can detect subtle energy, invisible to the naked eye. This "sight" enables them to perceive future events in dreams or visions. This is not to be confused with psychics or prophets. A psychic is a person with an inborn ability to occasionally see into future events. Prophets are individuals appointed by the Supreme Being due to their high level of righteousness. Believe me, a psychic is not always such a *tzaddik* (righteous person).

I was very young when I began to read futures for others professionally, peering into the future by just looking at a blank wall. However, this was very unsettling for people. Not wishing to scare them, I looked for a prop. Someone recommended I buy a tarot deck, so I did. At first, I would only pretend to look at the cards during a session. Over time, I actually began to study tarot and found that in almost any tarot deck you will find one symbol that remains constant in the depiction of the Priestess: the veil across the face of a seated woman. The veil represents the world of the unseen. The Priestess is a clairvoyant who lives between worlds, slightly detached from society. While this sounds alluring and mystical, when practiced, it generates for a lonely existence.

When I went into training at the meditation school and studied auras, I discovered I was also a clairaudient, a rarer form of clairvoyance in which information pertaining to reality is picked up via the sense of sound. I use a gong and play on the xylophone to hear the future. Messages come to me between the vibrational tones.

So I let go of the tarot prop and found something much better.

It is popular to romanticize psychic abilities, but it can be terribly hard, such as foreseeing a shattering event that one is powerless to prevent. This is why true psychics do not hang around bars or reality shows. Thoughts have a vibration that can be translated through different senses, and the noise and smell (all types of perception are possible) of people's thoughts is often too much for them. They typically prefer places like the woods or bookstores, where the vibrations are a little more soothing. For me, either the information comes in segments, like pieces to a puzzle or, if I am unable to pinpoint the exact date, just a rough timeframe in which things will occur. This is why I do not like to look into the future. But if I must, I am full of faith that the Eternal One decides our fate, and can change our future in a moment.

My life certainly testifies to this belief.

**Clairvoyant Eyes**

You can spot clairvoyants by the ring of dark blue or purple around the pupils of their eyes. I have been told my eyes take on a subtle violet cast with a greenish-gold ring during readings. This trait is not obvious, like an X-Men mutation, but a subtle one only noticed by careful observers. I once met a technology founder from India at a dinner party and as I was speaking with him I noticed purple markings around his irises. Though he appeared to be a very successful businessman, I asked him outright if he was clairvoyant. He paused for a moment, studied my eyes, and confirmed what I suspected. He told me when he was younger he had lived in the streets until he was found by a master. He studied and gained powers, which he used to help others until he became weary of the energy drain from serving the multitudes that came to see him. He began to develop serious health issues. He knew he could not continue like that and live, so he stopped. With many trials, hard work, and an uncanny knack for timing, he became a successful entrepreneur, now affecting others in the world of business. Nevertheless, the markings in his eyes always remained.

**Turning On Clairvoyance**

After years of practicing, I can now turn my clairvoyance on and off, like a light switch. This way, I take in as much information as I can within moments. It is the equivalent of taking a mental photograph of someone's aura—almost like its fingerprint. This takes tremendous focus—the equivalent of running 500 miles in five minutes. That would be something! The physical body would break down.

Clairvoyance connects to a body that you cannot see with your physical eyes. Seeing through time and space is both a gift and burden, between trying to maintain constant awareness and the emotional toll of such concentration. It is very disconcerting when people come up and abruptly ask me to read them, then and there. Equally disconcerting is when someone judges my ability or is fearful of it.

One may only look at another person's energy with his or her permission; to look without asking is impolite, like going through someone's purse. When I do a reading, I first pray that the Almighty will allow me to see this person. While some seers can activate clairvoyant abilities within others, I do not engage in this practice. These abilities may offer value, but they come at a price. Clairvoyant and clairaudient experiences can be as psychologically damaging as a bad reaction to a hallucinatory drug (like acid). It is hard enough to cope with everyday life—never mind multiple realities! Nor is there an effective method of preparation, even when you have the ability to see or hear things that others cannot. This is why I do not prioritize developing clairvoyance: the ability to see the future does not make for an easy life. Coping with this gift is a life-long adjustment.


**Intuition is Essential**
Intuition is a sixth sense that bridges matter and spirit. We cannot see, smell, or grasp it. This sense is inherent in everyone.
*What are the benefits?*

- When you develop your intuition, you will begin to see things as they are, rather than what you desire.
- Intuition builds self-confidence because you will be more in touch with your fundamental nature.

Intuition can save you from years of bad choices. It will help you get in touch with the essence of your soul's truth. Listening to your intuition will help you find that purpose when the world tells you otherwise.

When I left this world, there was nothing more I could do. I prayed to be returned, to get a second chance. I wanted to do more. Had I left for good, this book would not be here; you would not be reading this. So, if you can take away anything from this book, consider these questions:

- Why are you here?
- How do your actions affect others?
- Are they meaningful . . . positive?
- What will your legacy be?

**Intuition and Instinct**

Oftentimes, individuals confuse intuition for instinct. Both are inherent in everyone, although in different measures. Instinct will often make sense to you, while intuition will not. The following are some clear examples:

- 'My body is hungry. My body needs food. I should eat.' This is **instinct**. VS. 'I have a weird feeling. I should not eat this food. I have no idea why.' This is **intuition**.

- 'I have to pick up and move right now.' **Instinct** VS. 'I feel like I should go there, but I cannot explain how I know.' **Intuition**

Ideally, both abilities should work in synergy and both are needed to live a balanced life.


**Energy: Stay, Leave, or Learn**

Though most people cannot see auras, almost everyone can sense energy to a degree. Like when you meet someone and feel instantly repelled or attracted, though you cannot explain why. Or when you walk into a room and, within seconds, feel invigorated, relaxed, or drained. This means you are sensitive to the energy field surrounding that person or area. If you find yourself having a strong reaction to a person, place, or situation, take a moment to step back. Consider the following possible reactions. In order to better understand the nature of each reaction to energy, they are paired with their polar opposites:

- *Drawn* vs. *Repelled*
- *Uplifted* vs. *Drained*
- *Receptive* vs. *Closed off*
- *Neutral*
- *Anger*
- *Comforted* vs. *Uncomfortable*
- *Excited* vs. *Apprehensive*
- *Joyful* vs. *Saddened*

Generally speaking, when a person has a strong reaction to something, there is something for you to learn or to leave. The key is discernment. You must decide what you are feeling, and then search deep into yourself to discover *why* you are feeling this. Most of the time, your initial reactions are correct and tell you the truth about the situation. However, there are also times when the opposite is true. Perhaps the situation is something you were put in to deal with. That is why discernment, honest discernment of the situation and your innermost self, is key; it reveals our intuition! Life is not black and white. Often we make mistakes when we do not listen to our intuition. We need to learn to trust it which takes time.

Take me for instance, a psychic. I had exactly what I needed to spiritually nourish myself, right within reach, but I was too caught up trying to escape my destiny to appreciate its beauty. A sign of spiritual maturity is when you can reflect on your experiences and recognize the gifts that we might have discarded to the sidelines.

When you walk on a trail and come across animal droppings, must you step in them because they fall on your path? Or do you simply walk around? The same concept holds true for challenging people or places in life. You do not have to engage with something just because it is on your path. The greatest thing can be right in front of you, but if you are unprepared to receive it, you will shun or run from it.

## Energy-Phobic and Energy Addict

When I was training in the meditation school, it was very easy to fall into the traps of both. Common within the school, many of us went to great lengths to avoid circumstances deemed to have 'negative energy'. Instead, we participated only in those with 'positive energy'. By doing so, we could feed our insatiable desire for elevated vibratory experiences, or simply 'good vibes'. In reality, this meant we would avoid anything uncomfortable, going to great means to evade real growth. Some people even avoided their families. Our desire to run from this discomfort, while understandable, was not an effective long-term practice.

A better alternative is building your internal connection through kind acts, prayer, and purposeful living. Anyone can put into practice these three things and become stronger for it. You will see real growth and progress in your life.

### Tyger Teaching: Green, Red, Yellow light, Exercise through Scanning

Find a spot to sit quietly; face east. Literally pull up the situation to the front of your mind's eye, visualize it, preparing yourself to scan. Then, place the situation in three months, six months, and a year. See what signals come to you. Is it a **green light or red light? Or yellow**? Is there a particular point where any of these signals intensify or minimize? Do they seem to be convex with energy or concave? A lack of energy can mean the situation is not strong for you. When it seems full of life then it is positive. Follow accordingly.

### Yes or No in Acute Situations

Sometimes, you may find yourself in an acute situation, where there is no time to follow an exercise. In these circumstances where you must make an initial, quick decision based on your intuition, follow this set of Tyger teachings:

- Perhaps you are driving down a road and the energy **does not feel right**. You keep pushing it off, but the apprehension stays. Respect your feelings and find a detour.

- There is a specialist that you **do not feel right** about. You have a choice. Find someone else; get another opinion.

- You meet someone and immediately feel a strong sense of "**No**". Whether it is in relation to work, a social gathering, or even something educational, honor this feeling. Do not force the connection. Go elsewhere.

- A soldier instinctually senses that, despite the obvious dangers, they need to drive through a hazardous terrain. Even though they might want to do otherwise, they feel intuitively to "**Push through, push forward, do it**". Honor it; it might save a life. (This is true for civilians as well). I have worked with enough veterans that have always relayed their survival, in part, to listening to the "**Yes**" voice despite external forces.

- You develop a sense that you must check on someone/something—a neighbor, the gas, the front door, make a phone call (texts don't count). It's an inconvenient time, but you have this sense of urgency. This is a **Yes** Follow this intuition.

### Chronic Situations

The second type of situations are chronic, in which you have nagging feelings of **unease and apprehension** towards going forward with a situation, person, place, or thing. Conversely where despite the external obstacles, and self-doubt **you sense you are doing the**

**right thing**.  Under these circumstances, follow these Tyger teachings:

- The timing could be off.  So often, we force ourselves to do something because of external pressures or because of linear thinking (wanting to do things in a certain order), even when the timing is wrong and we need to wait.  In our world of instant response, with at our fingertips, we have forgotten the strength and wisdom of patience.  Life is curly; watch your expectations regarding yourself and others.

- You go to a certain location and always feel uncomfortable there; it never feels right.  There is something that makes you feel anxious.  **Pay attention**!  It might have nothing to do with, the structure itself, but the collective energy field present.  Should this feeling remain each time you visit respect this!  We are given warnings to our intuition not to make us crazy, but in order to take appropriate actions.

- A developer is about to build a complex on a piece of land.  The thought keeps coming to them **"I should not be doing this"**.  Experts have verified that all is well, the stats were exemplary; furthermore it is an excellent economic opportunity.  Pay attention to that intuitive feeling; it could be foresight of an event occurring that will hinder the success of the situation, be it external or internal.

- You feel a sense of calm and peace when you interact with a certain situation, person, or place.  Such as going to a particular class or workshop on continuing education or to learn a higher teaching.  Despite obstacles that might impinge you from going, do your best to attend. **Stay committed!** Real growth calls for strength and discipline which does not come without challenges.

Energy is the essence of everything. When we react to something, we may be reacting to its' essence, its' form, or perhaps both. So, what does the aura look like?

## The Aura

Auras are translucent sheaths that encapsulate the gross material dimensions of the body and contain the light emanating from the soul. Highly skilled clairvoyants can see this light, which varies in hue. Each color correlates to a particular vibration, which in turn has multiple effects on us that can be both positive and negative, both temporary and long-standing. Auras always exist and transmute continually according to our actions. When I read them, I am just peering into a moment to see. Within animals, I see energy surrounding and within their physical body. Though auras can surround plant life and inanimate objects, such as rocks and other minerals, I have personally only detected swirling energy centers around humans.

Auras may display information pertaining to a person's past, present, and future within concentrated swirling balls of light. In this book, I call these lights 'energy centers', but some traditions refer to them as chakras. A person's aura can fluctuate greatly depending on mood and situation, and auras do not age in the same manner as the physical body.

**Why Would an Aura Need Repair?**
Just like whatever our mouths consume affects our bodies, whatever our senses consume and whatever actions we take can affect our being. For instance: a person who misuses drugs, alcohol, or nicotine will have an aura that appears brownish-gray, with streaks in the chakras. These "streaks" are etheric tears, which leave an opening in the aura that can enable entry of negative energies. A few clients have ignored my instructions and took drugs the night before. I always know and refuse to give them a reading. The nature of these energies mutate and amplify desire to ingest the substance they feed off. Keeping the "host" addicted and on a vicious cycle until the "food" is cut off. Literally, one has to starve these energies from their source. Harmful actions create grayish wormlike shapes within the aura's shell, or worse, depending on the circumstances. Of course, these are extreme cases. We all have murky auras and congested chakras to various degrees. (Thankfully, I cannot see mine!)

Fortunately, there are ways to repair a damaged aura. I have personally seen the Psalms purify an individual's aura in moments. The Omnipotent speaks all languages, and consistently reading the Psalms over time can produce extraordinary results in one's life: transforming, repairing, and rebuilding the aura's light within and surrounding us. It is said the King David, the main author of the Psalms, knew the future and wrote the Psalms as a means of rectifying our souls pain. The Psalms are way to approach the Creator honestly, with our humanity. They cover the gamut of the human condition, which is why they are as pertinent today as they were thousands of years ago. The author, a powerful and holy king, reveals his imperfections before G-d, yet still asks for mercy, prosperity, wisdom, long life, and—especially—spiritual guidance. It is also important to know that King David came from converts and, like many of us; his family was not so perfect. He was chosen as king precisely because of his illustrious background, which lent him street cred and gave him the ability to relate to others. He faced and eventually triumphed over the inherent struggle every individual faces, being born with two very different souls in conflict with one another.

## Q and A with Tyger

*What do you do if your child sees auras?*

Babies can usually perceive auras. That's why a baby will react very strongly to different individuals. They are sensitive to energy, since they just came from the Ultimate Source. As they mature, they become curious to the world around them and they will begin to lose these abilities. If these abilities resurface, it is usually from the age of six to nine, where a child will say: "Mommy, I see lights around you". The best thing to do in cases such as this is to listen attentively. Be free to ask questions, but do not encourage or discourage. Just be present with them. Oftentimes, people will go to extremes in their reactions, denying the ability flat-out or feeding into it. The best course of action is to remain neutral and let the child express itself. If not careful, this ability can turn into a distraction and a crutch.

*What do you do if your child foresees future events?*

Again, follow the same steps as with the above question. With the modern overload of media and films and pop culture influence, there is a great lack of boundaries regarding psychic abilities. So, ask yourself these questions: *Are they trying to escape something, maybe school or peer pressure? Are they prone to fantasy? Perhaps they are not being challenged creatively?*

You need to develop more structure in their lives. Gently, let them know that they are in not in charge of these events. What they see might not necessarily happen. Distract them with something else. They need to learn how to tone their abilities down, and you will have to teach them how. I, personally, imagine a light switch being turned down to dim or even completely off. This will immediately calm down the nervous system and make them much happier. Seeing events can be overloading to all systems and can induce feelings of guilt when one is not mature enough to truly understand that there is really very little we can control in the world. It is far better to teach them self-mastery over their abilities.

*How can I tell if something is fear or a premonition?*

Fear will cause a physical response. Of course, fear can be a useful tool in protecting ourselves. I am not advising you to ignore your fears. There is a thin line between nagging feelings that something is not right as compared to something that engulfs you.

For practical purposes, should you develop such an overwhelming fear before you do something, pause. Elevate your awareness upwards to the areas around the top of your head, especially the areas above your ears and on the back of your head. Imagine that you have activated higher thought within you. If done correctly, this will immediately bring internal composure, if only for a few moments. Continue doing this exercise for three rounds. See if this helps your fears dissipate. Then, while you are in a composed state, decide what you have control over and what is out of your control.

Conversely, a premonition nags at you in quiet moments. There are many levels of premonitions; some everyone possesses, while others are gifts. Below are five main levels that I have encountered:

- *Déjà vu* --- You have a sense, but you are not certain
- *Intuition* --- Strong internal feeling
- *Dreams* --- When unadulterated, they facilitate a connection with your higher soul
- *Clairvoyance* --- Foresee events of future that free will can still alter
- *Clairaudience* --- You pick up information about the present or future via sound

It can be difficult to discern whether or not fear is a premonition. When we are fearful, our emotions are highly volatile and will block most of our intuition. I have found that saying the following psalms consistently will help bring clarity on this matter, in a lasting way.

- For acute situations --- Psalm 23,
- For chronic conditions --- Psalm 71

If you wish to refine and strengthen intuition, know that you are in it for the long haul. Activating and utilizing our intuition takes patience and practice; we have to grow into it. It is part of our spiritual development to even recognize that there are alternative choices available. When you are at a crossroads, use your intuition to engage your mind. I am a born clairvoyant and an expert in my field, and I can tell you right now that I am still working on it.Be patient, the more you train the intuitive muscles, the stronger they will become.

CHAPTER THREE

# How I Began to Study Energy

## Prints and Patterns of the Aura

At the age of twenty-two, I moved back to the United States, having already lived in several countries. Along my travels, I had met many eccentric characters, one of who became a close friend. Crazy as a bed bug and very creative, she was raised by her grandparents in Ireland when her parents ran off to India to live in an ashram. By the time I met her, she had seen it all, having travelled the world with her much older boyfriend, an aging poet and rock star. He had outlived most of his peers who died of drug overdoses; between binges of serious self-medication, my girlfriend helped him stay alive. She used all kinds of strange concoctions on him, from a variety of alternative therapies, and some of them actually worked. So when I began having health issues, she suggested I try this Master healer in L.A. I thought, *Why not?* So I went to Santa Monica, where the healer was giving an introductory workshop on energetic medicine.

As the class finished, Master M motioned to me and I saw what looked like green light shoot out of his hand. But When I asked him about it, he was shocked and began speaking a mile a minute, asking if I could see various other colors. After twenty minutes or so, Master M finally finished his examination. He suggested I meet own his teacher, Grand Master X, who was coming soon to the U.S. for a retreat. I remember thinking; *finally, someone will help me with my gift.*

After the retreat, Master M introduced me to the Grand Master so that he could test my abilities. The Masters brought me to a man and asked to relay what I saw. I concentrated on the man's aura and I saw the formation of tumors. I relayed this to Grand Master X. With a face betraying no emotion, he asked if I could pinpoint the location of the tumors. Without hesitation, I found the exact spots. The Grand Master smiled; this patient had previously brought his x rays to the Grand Master and they affirmed my report.

My training began immediately. Grand Master X was a beautiful person, the modern founder of a healing modality based on ancient energetic principles, with students from all over the world. His approach was similar to acupuncture, but without needles. A clairvoyant with the ability to see inside the body was incredibly useful for their research. In return, I trained with Grand Master X personally. He knew more about clairvoyants then anyone I had ever met. However, these lessons came at a heavy price.

As I studied energy, I learned to categorize the colors I detected in peoples' auras. There was a huge spectrum to work with. For instance, if I saw aquamarine light in the aura or corresponding energy center, I knew (even if they did not) that the individual possessed a healer's touch. When I saw violet around a person's crown, I knew they were clairvoyant. Red light, depending on the hue and location, indicated strong physicality and passion, which I usually saw around athletes and healthy adults. I focused intensely on my training for several years. My goal was to become an expert in this unique field of energetic healing; to ease people's suffering.

In a short time, word spread and people came from all over the world for readings. Soon, I became exhausted. In order to keep up with the demand, I would go to the masters for healings to remove the "negative" energy from my aura. These healings felt amazing, like taking a cool shower in a waterfall. I would feel peaceful and sleep deeply. In the following weeks and months, as the teachers intensified their meditations, the healing sessions grew "interesting." Once, after a lengthy healing, I went home to rest. In bed, with eyes closed, I suddenly saw Day-Glo wheels of light spinning inside my eyelids. Opening them did not help, and after only a few seconds I felt like my mind was going to break! In a panic, I put my forehead against X's back, and the images ceased immediately. Joseph is such a physical guy it, was like putting my head on the ground. This was the antidote necessary to pull me back from the hallucinations caused by the "healing."

The next day, I spoke with Master M. He informed me that the healing could have ripped the etheric web that protects the center connected to clairvoyance. The "shutter," normally closed, is an invisible sheath over the third eye. This protects a person from seeing the different worlds that exist alongside ours. I was fortunate that my "trip" did not last long, or damage me permanently. However, my amplified clairvoyant abilities—specifically, a hyperactive "antenna"—remained. Only after years of trying various techniques have I learned how to remain grounded in my clairvoyant abilities.

## Integrated Soul Workout: Nature Walks to Balance the Aura

It can be helpful to become mindful of your aura and how it affects reality around you. For example, I know I am in a peaceful place when butterflies occasionally land on my arm. You can develop this ability by practicing this simple exercise:

Go outside and take a walk. Observe how quickly birds move away from you or settle near when you sit. While we cannot see our own aura, animals can, and will respond accordingly. With practice, it may happen more often, unless they are disturbed by negativity in the surrounding environment.

Next time you see birds quickly fly away from you, take a moment to slow your gait and become mindful of your energy. Intentionally shift your energy by conjuring an uplifting thought or prayer will cause your auras frequency to also alter. This technique can facilitate awareness, respect, and more effective communication in every area of your life.

### Tyger Teaching: Walking for Connection

Negative energy can stick to us, accumulating from internal chatter or our external environment. In order to balance ourselves, we need to release this harmful energy. The most effective exercise I have found is also quite simple and anyone can use it:

Find a park or forest—even a quiet neighborhood will do. Take at least thirty minutes to walk, focusing your mind so that your thoughts do not drift. Consciously connect to the Higher Power to help purify you. Use the nature around you or the quiet as tools to help strengthen your connection. With each physical step you take, concentrate on rooting yourself to this world.

**Tyger Tip: Plugging In**

If you do not know how to connect to the Higher Power—perhaps you do not even believe in G-d, try and experiment. Think about these questions:

- How is it possible to have intuition?
- Who created intuition?
- If you believe in intuition, something that is invisible and hard to quantify, why not consider broadening that mindset?

## Activating the Flame of the Soul

When a person connects to prayer, I see gold and white light around the crown. In some cases, it may appear to have an ever-so-slight tinge of orange and a faint blue within it, like a flame. It can expand to several inches above the crown and might go all the way around the shoulders. In all my years of looking at people's auras, I have only seen one level of the soul, if any. (There are five levels, which we will not go into in this book.) Revealed to me unexpectedly, this *ruach,* which in Hebrew means 'air' or 'breath', appeared in a man I know. He was standing in front of me one evening, when suddenly, I saw the pure white air breathing within his torso. I was stunned! What the body usually concealed was revealed to me. Seeing this moving white air was a gift! Now, when this person pushes my buttons to the limit, I think back to this moment and appreciate his pure soul within. This helps me to remain elevated in my dealings with him. The trick is to hold this intention with everyone—judge everyone favorably and seek out his or her pure soul. If we all did it more regularly, imagine what the world would look like. Of course I am still working on this!

Whether we are aware of it or not, energetic areas around the head work like radio antennas, picking up frequencies of consciousness that can help us connect to higher planes or the reverse. This is why it is important to consider what your eyes look at, ears listen to, nose smells, and how your body behaves. When these areas are activated, and directed for good, unlimited human potential can manifest, physically and spiritually.

## Seeing Auras

There is a technical way and a spiritual way to see auras. I do not specialize in the technical way, and in my opinion, forcing this ability is unnatural and inadvisable, as it can lead to problems later on. To see auras spiritually takes much longer, but it is an authentic practice. If a person is going to see an aura, generally, it is when they least expect it and are not searching. When it does come, it only lasts for a few seconds. This is because the energetic muscle has not been conditioned.

If you cannot see auras, do not be discouraged, for that is not the only way to gain insight into human conditions. Energy vibrates in many different levels and forms, and those who pay attention can learn to intuitively read subtle shifts.

In order to view something spiritually, we must first repair ourselves spiritually. To that end, prayer offers us mental, emotional, and physical benefits so we feel greater peace and acceptance as we move up and down the ladder between the spiritual and the mundane. Which will continue throughout life. When we seek and create meaningful experiences in our lives reach emotional and spiritual depths we had not previously attained. This is part of the evolution of our soul. Know it is normal to have days where we are more balanced than others; the point is to know where you are going, and where you come from. I have a reminder on my desk that I composed to keep me focused. **"Remember who you are and where you intend to go. Be a light amongst nations, a daughter/son of King David, blessed be his name, believe in yourself, seek and embrace the good in life."** If you would like a more universal version of this saying, substitute **"A child of the Most High."**

## The Body's Energy Centers

For those who can perceive them, energy centers appear as etheric, swirling colored lights hovering over major organs and openings in the body. Highly skilled clairvoyants can pick up impressions regarding a state of an individual by assessing the quality, shape, and color of each *energy center*. (Some modalities refer to a similar idea, known as *chakras*.)

After studying thousands of people's energetic health for nearly twenty years, the findings described in this book are based on how I personally perceive energy running through energetic and physical bodies. We all have our subjective perceptions of reality; this is not an exact science, and nor is it meant to be. But I hope my experiences may be borrowed as a map to those looking to make their own way, and who wish to learn about auras and energy centers. I am thankful this research has enabled me to guide individuals to further the path towards true healing, whether by directly doing the spiritual work, by guiding them to medical and other therapeutic professionals for further evaluation, or by helping them discover their own healing frequency.

So often a person's physical discomfort can be traced to a lack of care for their spiritual souls. All stress-related illness stems from lack of understanding of the spirit within, as well as the body, that needs rejuvenation. If we approach disease from only a physical perspective, we will never fully heal. We should look at illness from a holistic approach and address the needs of the soul.

When working as a medical intuitive, I recommended further therapeutic investigation and support. When appropriate. But it took years of study and experience to learn to classify hues, patterns, and connotations, of energy alignment in the body's energy centers, and I looked at multiple cases for several years before I advised others.

Studies have found incorporating a spiritual as well as physical aspect to treatment is helping facilitate greater patient satisfaction and welfare. It used to be that a medical intuitive would be consulted as a last resort, when someone had not found relief or a satisfying diagnosis elsewhere. This is fast changing, due to the emergence of integrative medicine. I work with naturopathic as well as allopathic doctors excited about innovative possibilities in healing.

**The Human X-Ray**

As a medical intuitive, I initially assess the health—to the best of my abilities—of an individual's frequency. I have the client turn to the side so I can see how energy protrudes from their profile, something difficult to see if I look at them head-on. Auras and energy centers can be concave, convex, or somewhere in-between. However, it is better to look at an individual from back to front to see where they are holding, emotionally. For instance, when someone is stuck in the past, they will carry excess energy behind the heart. When I see this pattern, I work with the person on mindfulness exercises to help bring them into the present. Another pattern detectable in an aura is excess energy around the area of the solar plexus, which reveals an individual prone to exaggerated emotions and immaturity.

Once a person's picture is in front of me, I tune into what I see in my mind—usually a silhouette with geometric shapes swirling around it. If a specific location commands my attention, I zoom in with my eyes still shut. I do not diagnose; I refer people to medical specialists for further evaluation.

But my findings have always been confirmed.

For instance, I might see a blue light surrounding the left side of the neck, indicating a thyroid condition in which the gland is slow or blocked. If the light comes up red, it is inflamed. Benign tumors will appear as whitish lumps, and in cases of anemia, I see a pale red light circulating throughout the body. I can detect diabetes or difficulties with blood sugar by a whitish, sticky-looking light in the blood stream.

It is very difficult to diagnose oneself, though I have at times been successful. For example, though nothing was found in an MRI scan of my brain, my being sensitive to light and sound, plus the headaches and fatigue, led doctors to diagnose me with multiple sclerosis. I knew intuitively they were incorrect. As I was too young for a colonoscopy, my intestinal complaints were dismissed as irritable bowel syndrome or gluten sensitivity. Frustrated, I began to ice the right side of my colon in the exact location the slow-growing tumor was found years later. I suffered like this for several years, with frequent trips to the emergency room, where blood in my stool was attributed to eating beets. Thanks to my work as a medical intuitive, I never gave up hope or belief that I would eventually recover.

I have seen unbelievable situations where people had overcome unbeatable odds. The following story is my favorite illustration of this point.

**The Case of the Miracle Baby**
Many years ago, a successful young man in the entertainment industry came for a consultation regarding his career. I pointed out some choices he had not yet considered. The session went well and he emerged from it seemingly energized.

A few days later he rang me, very upset. His sister-in-law, who was almost six months pregnant, had received disturbing news: multiple tumors had been detected around the brain and spine of her fetus. The doctors surmised the baby was deeply deformed and unlikely to live more than a few days, should the pregnancy even go to full term. Because of these findings, a team of doctors and professionals recommended a late-term abortion. My client was frantic. This was to be the first grandchild born to his close Greek family. He asked if I could look into the situation clairvoyantly.

Obliging, I closed my eyes, and saw a boy around age two, in complete health. I relayed this to my client, who excitedly passed the message on to his family. But a few days later he called back disheartened: a third ultrasound had revealed even more tumors then the previous two! The family, deeply saddened, made arrangements for the procedure to take place and to support the couple's decision as best as they could.

I was puzzled. Once I was off the phone, I prayed and closed my eyes. I saw the boy as a toddler again, clapping his hands, surrounded by a golden aura in seemingly perfect heath. I immediately called my client back and insisted that they do one last ultrasound. The family gathered for an emergency prayer session and the next morning requested one last ultrasound, just to be sure they were doing the right thing. The medical practitioner obliged, expecting the same results as the previous three tests.

The fourth and final ultrasound revealed a perfectly healthy male fetus with no evidence of abnormality. A true miracle had taken place, and a healthy boy was born three and half months later.

As this story suggests, I specialize in seeing children before they are born. I think it is because I love to be joyful—and what is more joyful than new life? Once, I was speaking with a friend whose first child was a girl I had seen before she was conceived. While we were chatting, suddenly, I had a vision of her father, who had died twelve years previously, playing with my friend's future son. They were laughing and sharing secrets. The boy seemed about four, with light brown curly hair and hazel eyes. The vision shifted and I saw her father standing over a baby, in a crib who looked up and smiled. My girlfriend had known me a long time and was not surprised. Later that day she rang me back, excited. While on the phone with her sister on the East Coast, she shared what I had seen. Her sister became quiet. That day she had been at her wits end. Her baby would not stop crying and there was nothing she could do; she was so tired, sat down and cried along with her. Suddenly, she felt the presence of her father in the room. Her baby looked up and began to laugh and gurgle. She had not only felt him, but she seemed to see him. The sisters realized this took place at the same time I was seeing the vision of the future and present moment. Two years later, my friend gave birth to her second child; a boy with hazel eyes who grew to have curly light-brown hair.


## Auric Archetypes and Patterns

Kabbalah teaches that seeing color is a blessing. Could we comprehend the infinite colors and worlds that live within ours, it would be far too overwhelming. While we should only perceive four dimensions (time being one of them), throughout thousands of years of history, people have reporting experiencing and witnessing mystical events that seem to go beyond the limitation of a fourth dimension. This has led to much speculation and curiosity in diverse fields of science, religion, art, and others by those who wish to explore the causes of what we know intuitively to be true. There is more to the world than meets the naked eye.

Though an aura's size, dimension, and color changes frequently depending on our mood, health, and activities, every individual possesses a base color that dominates their archetype. The following are four core archetypal patterns and hues. (There are more than four archetypes that I have seen, but for the scope of this book, I have grouped a few of them together). Observe yourself and note when you find yourself leaning towards one category more than others. Below are some examples from years of personal investigation into the space around and within our physical and emotional bodies and how this can affect us.

### The Mentalist: Innovator of Thought

*Predominant color: yellowish-gold*

*Gifts: Ability to quickly detect patterns, to formulate theories, and to formulate strategies that benefit mankind*

In the Mentalist archetype, individuals have an auric pattern where, compared to the rest of the body, moderate-to-high energy pools collect between the eyebrows, forehead, and back of the head. They are highly analytical and best suited to work in strongly scientific fields, like technology or research. In extreme cases, the mental powers are so consuming that the emotional and instinctive nature appears underdeveloped and concave. If he were real, the character of Sherlock Holmes would be a good example of this pattern.

Unchecked, the effects of this energetic pattern can create blockages in the heart, navel, and sex centers, which reduces a person's empathy, appetite, and power to relate to others in a physical manner. Often, I see these conditions in people with Asperger's syndrome. To break this pattern, I direct the person to connect to the upper energy centers and their body through music—whether by learning to play an instrument, listening to recordings, or attending concerts.

Mentalists also benefit from exercise outdoors, where the colors and frequencies specific only in nature refresh and rejuvenate the emotional and physical body, allowing the intuitive soul to emerge from the grips of the mind that has gone into overdrive. I can personally attest to several cases where these individuals, by taking weekly Sabbaticals from technical stimuli and trading it for time in nature, grew more in touch with others and with their intuitive feelings.

The color yellow is strongly connected to the mind and the solar plexus, which governs the ego. When it this is operating from a healthy frequency it boosts analytical and observational skills, self-confidence, and ambition, rather than unhealthy, narcissistic behavior.

Related: Founders and corporate CEOs also carry strong energy between their eyebrows. However, unlike the Mentalist, there is a greater connection to, and significant enlargement of energy around the throat, solar plexus and sexual areas, lending enhanced speaking and leadership qualities. On the other hand, the Mentalist—though more brilliant then most—needs assistance with implementation of vision.

Here's a tip: When you assemble a team for some purpose, before you decide on which members to include, see if you can feel for the energy center that dominates a potential member's frequency. Determining this will lend greater understanding of their strengths and limitations, and whether they will work within the scope of your organization or plan. (Or, of course, you can call me and I will take a look for you.)


**The Athlete: Transformation through Physicality**
*Predominant color: red to magenta*
*Gifts: Possessing inherent physical courage; when channeled in a healthy manner, they are great protectors of humanity, animals, and the earth; connects to spirituality through physicality, elevated potential, and integration of soul and matter*

People blessed with the gifts of the Athlete have the most potential to attain the greatest spiritual heights out of all the archetypes. Why is this? Possessing a stronger affinity for physical matter, they struggle less to understand and relate to the material world. Should the raw energy that circulates throughout these individuals be directed for good, they can transform reality. Examples of this are firemen, and all the search-and-rescue, protective forces, and emergency medical teams and people that work with the body.

No amount of technology can substitute for basic health. We have incarnated in bodies that achieve optimum effects when they are healthy. This is why individuals who fall under the athlete archetype can do such good for the world—especially when they join forces with the Spiritualist and Mentalist. The Athlete's biggest challenge is facing the incessant demands of their inner animal desires, which buries the needs of their spiritual soul. The body becomes a major distraction, preventing them (or anyone) from engaging the mind, the state where intuition is downloaded as a language understood by the soul. This physicality makes them impulsive with their actions and decisions. Like a trained lion, if you place catnip in front of the Athletic, you had better move out of the way. These individuals have the quickest response to physical stimuli. Unless they work with their intuitive soul, their instincts will take over.

All archetypes have their own catnip that will set them off. When we connect to our minds and spiritual nature, we rise above the level of instinct; we become less reactive.

The solution for balancing the Athlete archetype is commitment to a daily spiritual practice; immersion in water (a paddleboard is great for this type) along with weekly study (astronomy, the intuitive arts, meditation, and nature) will feed their spirit and make them less reactive and agressive. For instance, my Pilates teacher falls into this archetype, yet she has a strong spiritual practice and studies the intuitive arts. Her predominate aura has a magenta hue, in contrast to the cherry red of many athletes. The magenta is close in range to purple, which is intuitive, carrying the calming effect of blue.

When the Athlete balances their animal and spiritual sides, they can become powerful. For instance, we have seen NFL players fall on one knee and pray before a game in front of millions of people. When was the last time anyone did this in such a public way before a meeting in Microsoft? People assume big guys like this have tremendous egos. In fact, some of the biggest egos I have worked with come in oddly small packages. Believe it or not, I have met Athletes who can create deeper and lasting connections to others than the Mentalist. Their inherently loving nature acts as a gateway to the spiritual soul.

**The Spiritualist: Connector of Worlds**
*Predominant colors: Purple, blue, green; at high levels, also whitish-gold and whitish-blue*
*Gifts: Intuitive discernment, empathetic nature; they are gifted communicators to humans, animal, plants, and minerals, which thrive in their presence and care due to the healing light that emits naturally from their aura*

The Spiritualist is a healer with a pronounced auric color and shape. An authentic leader who has worked extensively refining themselves will hold tremendous energy around the head and shoulders. This energy appears white with hints of gold, blue, or violet.

An auric pattern of light envelops the entire length of their bodies, radiating out several inches or even feet from the body. For clairvoyants, this light is detectible even when their heads are covered.

In the presence of Spiritualists, others will feel soothed and comforted. When they speak, you can hear the empathy. Their internal compass always goes back to their true North, and this is expressed in their unending desire to help others and improve the world.

At the highest level, their actions, even the most mundane, are done for elevated purposes: they eat in order to give thanks, they keep the body healthy in order to function properly, and they live in order to fulfill their purpose of incarnation. Even their sexuality will be channeled in an elevated manner to an experience of Divine union, instead of just personal pleasure. They perceive the connections between spirit and matter. Their clairvoyance is of no interest to them personally, unless it can be used to serve others.

The challenge for individuals of this archetype is to remain balanced in their bodies, from which they are detached. They have this in common with the Mentalist, who cannot be interrupted to deal with the demands of the body (I know of a couple Mentalists who would rather be fed with an IV so long as they could continue working on their computers). However, for the Spiritualist, this detachment derives from a deeper perception and acute sense of the soul's longing to be with her Creator.

Due to the Spiritualist's intimate nature with higher levels of the soul, if they are put in situations when they feel disconnected with the Source or their sensitivity is challenged, they will feel physical discomfort. How can we fix this problem? Look to the wise words of J.K. Rowling.

*"Happiness can be found even in the darkest of times, if one only remembers to turn on the Light."*
Albus Dumbledore

If these individuals fail to connect to the Light, they have the potential to fall harder into darkness than anyone. Our story traditions are full of these examples, such as Jean Grey, a superhero in the X-Men series. Because of the level of her clairvoyance, she is considered the most powerful character of all.

In the initial stories, Jean Grey's abilities are the most helpful to Professor X's quest to help humanity. However, once she is swayed to darkness by her own free will, those same gifts are used to destroy the Professor and anyone that stands in her path. This continues until, in the midst of the chaos, she asks to be killed in order to prevent additional harm. Of course, this is fiction, and an extreme example of psychic powers far outside our reality. However, in rare cases where people do have exceptional abilities and powers, the lesson holds: **abilities should never be taken for granted**. As light and darkness sit beside each other, the fall affects others greater and hurts harder from the mountain than the floor.

I have found that people whose predominant aura color is blue, green, turquoise, or purple often work in the profession of healers, therapists, clairvoyants, social workers, arborists, animal communicators, herbalists, and so on. In order to recharge this type needs plenty of time resting, at least eight hours of sleep a night. They thrive in environments that match their sensitive nature. Should they not learn to set boundaries and stay grounded, they will have a hard time operating in mundane reality. Without a spiritual discipline and commitment to a meaningful practice these individuals may isolate, have difficulty earning a living or succumb to recreational drugs. Alternatively, this archetype can play in everyone else's narrative, trying single-handedly to save the world.

*"If I am not for myself, who will be for me?*
*But when I am only for myself, what am I? And if*
*not now, when?"*
Hillel the Elder

For Spiritualist archetypes I recommend they print this quote and place it somewhere they can see it every day.

Other solutions that help balance this group is to physicalize, whether swimming, working out in a gym, practicing Pilates, or walking in the forest. These are all grounded activities. Another terrific remedy to strengthen the Spiritualist is working with children and socializing with others, at least once a week. This healthy and protective strategy helps to build spiritual immunity more effectively than isolation.

**The Artist: Inspiration**
*Predominant colors: Much like the artist themselves,*
*mutable and multicolored*
*Gifts: To inspire and empower others through their*
*creativity, invoking light through the gates of joy and*
*the laughter of entertainment*

The aura of the Artist is not as defined as the others in a particular color. The area around the throat, solar plexus, naval, and sexual center is convex, with energy pooling excessively in these locations compared to the rest of the body. These patterns lend individuals an inherent desire to express themselves. When they are balanced and spiritually connected, they can be a tremendous source of inspiration to the world at large. Like the Spiritualist, they can be highly effective in reaching the hearts and minds of others, their energy is naturally effusive. Unlike the Spiritualist, they seek and need attention from others in order to feel alive. This desire, coming from having an overactive solar plexus in the aura, lends the Artist confidence to perform. Think of how most of us feel about public speaking. Imagine performing in front of 60,000 people—this is an energy that wants to be noticed! It is big, expansive, and even motivational. Yet without direction and will power, this energy can become very destructive.

Artistic vision has helped to change the course of history, inspiring others to reach and dream higher. And many of these visionaries have been challenged by their overactive solar plexus, which can lead to emotional instability. Ultimately, this leads to self-medication and other escapist tendencies in an attempt to fill the empty hole. In turn, the artist goes further and further away from fulfillment. The best protections: Daily routine and commitment to prayer and meditation, which lifts a person out of their needs of their ego, and into awareness of their soul. This includes chores (no one is too powerful for them, period). Thru giving humbly, the Artist learns to channel their charisma to motivate, not denigrate. The Mentalist and Artist can learn many things from one another, hence the well-established relationship between agent and performer, for example, which falls in this category.

## Auras and Health

The following are some physical conditions that I have seen appear in the aura:

- Diseased energy will appear in the aura as a muddy brown color, with streaks of dark red and a sticky appearance and texture.
- Benign tumors may appear as white forms; otherwise they may present as shades of reddish, brownish-black.
- Blood disorders such as diabetes appear as white, sticky energy circulating throughout the body.
- Hypertension will correspond to a tight, red aura around the tailbone, as well as various red hues circulating throughout the body.
- When woman are menstruating, the naval, sex, and coccyx will appear swollen and the colors faded. This is also true for pregnant women, though with vastly different hues. In healthy pregnancies, the aura will emit deep emerald, rosy pink, and golden tones.
- People with a highly active sex energy centers hold excessive energy in the throat, navel, and sexual center. Their aura will look like a bell.

### The Effect of Emotion on the Aura

- *Unadulterated love:* Two individuals in love have a combined, intertwined aura that looks akin to an impressionist painting. Hues of whitish turquoise, whitish pink, and other pastels are blended together. Everyone can sense when this aura is present, because the energy it exudes is vibratory and uplifting. This also is true for a mother and her child, especially during nursing years. Any moments of tenderness between individuals can also have a similar aura.

- *Synergistic energies:* When individuals are communicating as a team and working effectively together, their auras merge and energy easily flows between them. Through this, they can easily influence one-another and learn from each other.

- *Aggressive energy:* When individuals struggle and fight with one-another, their auras separate and can even become jagged like darts. This is why aggression repels sensitive individuals. Such energy is palpable. When people or animals are aggressive, their whole aura appears tight, muddy, and reddish-brown.

- *Spiritual energy:* When an individual is praying with intention, their aura instantly becomes a circle of light. The color remains white with hints of blue, gold, or sometimes purple.

- *Competitive energy:* The aura is cherry red with yellow sheen, in the formation of a moving wall. Often seen in athletes, especially high-level athletes.

- *Repressed energy:* If a person is holding energy, the location will appear tight or lacking in energy. For instance, if an individual is afraid to speak, the area around the throat will appear depleted and tight. The same is true for people who withhold from others: Misers on any level—be it emotional, spiritual, or financial—will have low energy and a weak aura that appears congested.

Why? Because it takes more energy to remain blocked than to open and flow.

- *Highly emotional energy:* People who are very emotional will hold energy in their solar plexus, navel, and behind the heart; these areas will appear convex or concave between the eyebrows, forehead, and above the head. I have frequently seen this energy in those with weight-management issues. An overactive nervous system can make it impossible for a highly emotional person to keep weight on or take it off.

- *Angry energy:* Anger is one of the most harmful energies to every aspect of existence. The sages tell us that our spiritual soul, which connects to our intellect, departs when we are enraged, leaving our animalistic nature unbound without reason. This temporarily severs the connection with our higher nature. "Seeing red" is literally more accurate than people realize.

- *Excessive anger:* Those dealing with prolonged anger—stifled or otherwise—tend to have issues in their unresolved history. Unresolved anger pools between the shoulders, the back of the heart, and the lower spine. The crown forehead space between the brows and heart will appear concave. The effects of anger left unchecked are so great that it can create an opening for negative forces to possess us.

- *Impulsive energy:* Impulsive people have fullness around their solar plexus, navel, and coccyx, with a concave area around the eyebrows. This is from persistent time spent in reactive mode without engaging the mind.

- *Deceitful energy:* When a person lies, their aura blinks. Akin to a power outage, they are temporarily disconnected from the Source.


**Energetic Properties of Color**

What is color? Color is how we perceive the reflection of light. On a deeper level, color is a way in which the Creator expresses beauty in this world. Every hue in the divine palate corresponds to energy of the Divine Architect's expression in creation. A fingerprint, if you will, of the artist of all artists.

Color affects our reality. By surrounding yourself with certain colors, you can activate and influence your sensory experience. Auras represent characteristics and potentials of an individual's soul. In order to understand what a person's aura means, we must understand the significance of each color and shade. Individuals with certain aura colors tend to embody these qualities and work in particular fields (colors are organized from higher to lower):

- *White:* connected to their spiritual soul; signifies purity, holiness, and innocence; white can denote the *Shekinah* (feminine aspect of G-d)
  - Spiritual teachers and leaders, Kabbalists
- *Gold:* Active engagement with the Highest Level of knowledge; seek to benefit humanity
  - Heads of spiritual schools, artisans of spiritual items, gifted classical or relgious musicians
- *Silver:* A very specific, high-level color. I will not go into it in this book.

- *Purple:* Intuition, knowing, and clairvoyance; refinement, musical abilities (especially the voice), and mature sensitivity
  - o Psychics, painters, opera singers, poets
- *Violet:* Similar to purple; likes to play with imagination rather than reality; mysterious
  - o Artists, actors and musicians have hints of violet
- *Blue:* Protection, mercy, and courage; excellent doctors and teachers; these individuals seek tranquility; very moral—highly value truth and honesty; remain calm under duress; in excess, can mean emotional distance
  - o Teachers, public speakers, army medics, gifted doctors, nurses, psychologists, EMT driver, NOT politicians
- *Turquoise:* A very specialized color; compassionate, gifted at communicating—especially with animals and children; highly artistic and creative; in excess, hints at difficulty connecting to earthly responsibilities
  - o Work with people with special needs like deaf and blind and autistic individuals. Animal communicators
- *Green:* Middle colors—signifies healing and growth; Bright green indicates loving kindness, healing, growth, and compassion; murky green indicates greed, illness, jealousy; in general—green auras denote a green thumb
  - o Physiotherapists, acupuncturists, herbalists, naturopaths, horticulturists
- *Pink:* Hope, romantic love, and innocence (to lesser degree than white, due to its connection to physicality)

- o More of a characteristic than a job—think of ten-year old girls
- *Yellow:* Intellect; ability to analyze and decipher information; strategy, especially involving numbers and technology; excessive detachment from emotions, environment, and circumstances
    - o Writers, lawyers, public speakers, technology, doctors, researchers, accountants
- *Orange:* Jovial, humorous, creative
    - o I have never seen anyone with just an orange aura
- *Red:* Strong physicality and sexuality, healthy body and circulation, passionate, instinctually courageous and protective; emotional; excess red means prone to excessive anger and selfishness; it can be dangerous, especially in dark hues with streaks or tears
    - o Police, firemen, nurses, dancers, soldiers, athletes

**Color Combos**

The following are examples of certain color combinations and the jobs that align with it.

- *Murky yellow and red*
    - o Majority of modern individuals due to technological addiction
- *Yellow, orange, and red* signify colors related to matter. These aspects of the aura relate to more physical drives and analytical natures
    - o Anthropology, surgeons, chefs (hints of green), intelligence agents, army personnel, businessmen, actors (hits of violet), announcers (hints of blue)

- *Yellow, red, and hints of gold*
  - Pilots
- *Green and yellow*
  - Nutritionists, winemakers
- *Gold with bits of blue and a little red*
  - Yogis
- *Green with purple hints*
  - Flower arrangers, aroma therapists
- *Various combinations*
  - Travelers, famous rock stars
- White with hints of yellow or blue
  - Babies and toddlers

When a girl hits age 12 and a boy hits age 13, their aura changes colors. This occurs again in a person's twentieth year (although it can be earlier).

It is not practical—nor is it safe—to see auras all the time. For my sanity, I have learned to turn my ability on and off. Without diligence, one can lose hold of reality, like a permanent psychedelic trip. Reading auras is a fast, slippery slope to becoming delusional, at best. So wield this ability carefully and spend time developing a sense of when to take a time out.

## Heaven (Not Stones) Opens Our Eyes

Some esoteric schools believe a clairvoyant should wear a ring (and sometimes more than one) to enhance their psychic abilities. These rings are considered talismans, or amulets, and are not to be touched by anyone else after they are crafted, lest the frequencies from others alter the stones' vibrations.

My rings now lie on the floor of the lake near the wetlands by my home. Eight weeks after my resection, I tossed them into the water. Having parted with flesh, I could detach from gems. I was in essence being reborn and had no use for them anymore.

A few years before, I had gone with Master X to the beach at night, while three other students and his wife waited for us in the car. He wanted to speak with me alone. We walked on the sand and he paused. He took off his ring and gave it to me to hold. The energy was too strong, and not right for me; I immediately became dizzy. Master X took the ring back, touched my shoulder, and then asked me to look at the water.

I saw the ocean was rough and turbulent. A vision appeared before my eyes that I could not decipher, with flags from various nations, symbols of banks, wars, floods, earthquakes, famines, and other terrible events. I saw that Master X had passed. I closed my eyes and began to cry. He quietly asked me what I saw, and what year the events would take place. My heart was racing and I felt sick but I had been trained to report. He reminded me that the future is not definitive, and that karma is complex. That if events were being advertised, events could alter.

Thankfully, not all of those events have taken place, but Grand Master X did leave this world at the young age of fifty-four. I have seen him a few times since, in dreams.

No matter what I did or not see, what is important to know is this: Divine decree can overturn any premonition or vision, and no one can predict the hour of death. We have been given free will to choose, but our past, present, and future is in the hands of Heaven.

CHAPTER FOUR

# Soul Mates

*"From every human being there rises a light
that reaches straight to heaven, and when two
souls that are destined to be together find each
other, the streams of light flow together and a
single brighter light goes forth from that united
being."*
Baal Shem Tov

Kabbalah teaches that forty days before you were conceived, your match was declared in *Shamayim* (Heaven). Until you join together, your souls long for each other. If this is true, why is it so hard to find The One? Or even to stay in a relationship for any meaningful length of time?

Our ego's needs are transitory and empty, like zero calories that leave you hungry and wanting more, creating a vicious cycle. As such, we often put ourselves in situations with others without considering our intentions or integrating our hearts and minds, thereby causing entanglements. The current lack of boundaries in modern culture has degenerated into such a state that we lend greater consideration to the rise of our jeans than with which we share our most intimate self. How can we prevent this? By reframing the mindset that comes from being misinformed and refocusing our priorities to what is lasting.

A soul mate is a connection based on the spiritual level. This book teaches how to understand and develop a relationship with your spirit. By focusing on developing your intuition, you will begin to relate to others on a higher level, which will align you to your other half.

## Do's and Don'ts for Attracting Your Soul Mate
- Act how you want to be treated. Require that you be treated with respect and dignity.
- Women often feel that they must meet the male at his level. This is **absolutely incorrect**. Oftentimes, a female soul will incarnate to help elevate her male counterpart, so it is essential that she maintain her integrity.
  - o If a woman continuously dates a man she know won't commit, she is enabling him to stay emotionally and spiritually stunted. Only in commitment can a couple grow past their comfort zone.
- If you want a *soul* mate, know that you will not find one by focusing on materialism (i.e. what they will give you). Instead, prioritize what it would mean to *build* a life together.

### Characterization of Entanglement
It can be hard to distinguish when you are in a positive, beneficial relationship or entangled in downward spiral. Ask yourself these questions:

*Do they distract you from your authentic purpose?*

*Do you share mostly hedonistic experiences?*
*Does being together create chaos in your life?*
*Is their main attraction for you physical?*

*Are they involved with others simultaneously?*
*Was your meeting willful or egocentric in nature?*
*Is there any meaningful spiritual growth?*
*If this relationship remains as it is for the next*
*five, ten years, will you be fulfilled?*

### Characterization of a Soul Mate

While reading the list, compare these points to a past or present romantic endeavor to help determine your patterns and choices in partners.

- A soul mate, more than likely, is a person you least expect. Your soul mate helps to complete your soul and will match your personality and spirit in ways you might not have anticipated or prepared for.

- Although your backgrounds, personalities, tastes and hobbies may be dissimilar, the core values remain congruent. A soul mate will attract meaningful experiences and your combined forces contribute positively to the world and align you to purpose. Your light is revealed when you are together; it is obvious to those around you, almost palpable. (Take a few pictures: can you see your souls shining between you, or are they buried?) It is obvious the Divine Providence put you together.

- With a true soul mate, any challenges in the relationship will help you to grow into your authentic self. Your soul mate does not join nor enable your ego be in charge. Instead kicks your *tuchas* (your butt) so you can be the man or woman you were meant to become.

- You will respect and trust one another to commit to keep the bond sacred. If mistakes are made, you work on repairing them
- Soul mates can have significant challenges they face. A hidden blessing to help them grow.
- Soul mates help each other to complete unfinished business from past incarnations.

**Know Your Nature**
Whether you are in a relationship or not, you have arrived where you are because of your past choices and patterns. Even if you are unhappy with your current situation, do not act with haste. This chapter as a whole is to encourage awareness in your life and relationships.

Time for some personal inventory and assessment to organize your mind! I am sure you have heard about "manifesting" your reality. While there is truth in this concept, if it were that simple, everybody would receive everything they wanted as soon as they wrote it down on paper. If the reality you have tried to create has not yet materialized, stop judging yourself! Reality is more complex than this. That being said, the purpose of this exercise is to align your mind. If you approach this with discernment, you will see whether or not your current desires are a fantasy or actually what is best for you.

What we all need is a kind soul, loving heart, and a strong mind aligned to a moral code of conduct. This combination will weather any stone. But first, we have to be that person ourselves.

For this exercise, write down the values and core beliefs that are important for you to have in your life. If loyalty is one of them (as it should be), a playboy, no matter how handsome or generous, will not make a happy match for you. Perhaps, you are all about the checklist. Even if they fit every box on your list does not mean you will fit theirs. If you are looking for perfect—remember, being around such an individual will only lead to insecurity. By the way, I have never met perfect. It is our flaws that make us unique and beautiful.

**Tyger Teaching: Mirage or Oasis**
What are you running towards? Make a list of qualities you would like in a partner. Beware of going on physical attraction, the size of the wallet, or even age. This is the yakking of your instinctual nature. Meaning, this is your animal soul expressing its will and desires. You can do better things with your time in life than to waste energy with those who will be just bedmates as opposed to a true partner. Be patient. Keep your eye on the goal of being with a soul mate. Physical attraction can wax and wane. Anything can change in an instant: young people can leave the earth (G-d forbid) before their parents, people age differently, fortunes can be lost, etc. The most important aspect, crucial to a happy relationship, is shared core values. So ask yourself:

- *Are they kind?*
- *Are they brave?* So many people will not make a commitment because of paralysis by analysis. Give the timid and intellectual a shelf date. Life is too short.
- *Do they make you laugh?* Sour pusses, no matter how intelligent or successful, make hot days and frigid evenings even longer.

- *Are they available?* I have consoled enough people over enough years, to tell you this: even if that person supposedly fits you like a glove, if they are married, they are not your soul mate. Remember, the ultimate matchmaker is the Creator, who does not take kindly to people's interference. To come between couples is both egocentric and disrespectful. Not only that, as a relationship between man and wife is likened to that between man and G-d; if you interfere, if can cause a Heavenly backlash. If you are absolutely convinced the married person is your true destiny, then let the Master of the World decide the matter. It is not your business to determine the outcome. Be a *mensch.* Have integrity; have honor! Do not walk, *run* away from the pit.

## Becoming Cognizant of Your Nature

Our hedonistic culture encourages us to act on our desires, without boundaries. How many of us engage in sexual relations to fill a hole in our lives or because we crave attention? Then we wonder why we feel isolated and lonely. In my work counseling others, I have yet to see a promiscuous person who is content with life. Then again, what is considered promiscuity by today's standards? On the other side of the spectrum, those individuals who give in only to their spirituality and ignore the needs of their body are equally impoverished. I witnessed and experienced this challenge heavily when I was in the meditation school.

Before we can embark on a soul mate relationship, it is important to develop a level of spiritual maturity within ourselves that has nothing to do with age. We can tell where we are holding on this by answering the following questions:

*Do you want your core relationship to have longevity and a legacy? Are you seeking experiences of meaning in your life? Are you willing to give of yourself 100%?* If you answered 'no' to any of these questions, you are not ready, nor looking for a soul mate. So don't tie up someone who is.

Kabbalah teaches that when Adam was formed, he saw that every animal in creation had a mate but man, and asked why he had no mate. So, woman was created from man as his partner, in Hebrew, referred as 'ezer kenegdo'. 'Ezer' translates to 'helpmate'. 'Kenegdo' has many meanings, integral to the nature of woman's relationship to man. It can mean 'opposite of', 'next to', 'opposing', etc. At the optimal state, the male and female are in balance with each other and she stands next to him, side by side. However, when they are out of alignment with their souls purpose, the energetic flow between them shifts. Rather than functioning as a partnership or one whole, they become two separate entities, opposing one another.

## Realizing Your Blocks

There are basic factors that hold people back. In order to recognize which might be affecting you, follow this exercise. Your answers might surprise you.

- Step one: Make two lists.
    o *Why you want a soul mate.*
    o *All that is stopping you from being with someone.*

Be honest in this self-inventory. Write down what comes to you immediately; do no overthink this! Most of the time, you will find that you are blocking yourself through your environmental influences and personal misconceptions.

- Step two: Answer these questions.
  - o *In your free time, where are you most often?*
  - o *Who are you generally with—single people, couples, or families?*
  - o *What is the nature of your surrounding influences?*
  - o *How open are you to that which makes you uncomfortable?*
  - o *How often do you read inspired teachings?*
  - o *Do you feel that you will change for the* right *one?*
    - ▪ This is a fallacy. The longer you practice a habit, the more it becomes entrenched behavior. So even if you temporarily can change, you will eventually return to your habitual nature. So change your patterns now.
- Step three: Say psalm 147 every day. Keep this up as long as you can.
- Step four: Give to charity **weekly**, on the same day every week if you can.

Done consistently, this exercise effectively and efficiently releases energetic blockages that may have developed over time and be preventing you from finding your soul mate.

**Tyger Teaching: Make a *Shidduch* (Match)**

Give that which you seek. Make a list of single people you know. Would any of them benefit from meeting? Is there a potential match between individuals? If so, make an introduction. Set a goal to check in periodically for the next three months to see if you can add or subtract from the list. In doing this, you are setting up a network of possibilities. Perhaps, in turn, someone else will consider you. It could be possible that you have overlooked someone you've met previously, or vice versa. The most important advice I can offer is something I am still learning: judge others favorably.

Always remember that your relationship is in the hands of the Supreme Being. I know of a couple who married at the age of forty-nine and were fifty-four when they had their first natural born child. Do not give up hope. Do not give in to despair. We are meant to continue praying for a soul mate. Commit to activities to keep inspired and remain joyful. This will cause the energetic channels and gates to remain open, when you least expect it, for your soulmate to come through. Remember, they are looking for you too, so, keep the light on!

CHAPTER FIVE

# Soulful Spaces

*I looked to the east, as I stood at the banks of the shore. The leviathans were breeching amidst the turbulent waters. One glided towards me, where it rested in the shallows. I waded in to touch its silver skin, which gleamed in the sunlight. It felt like velvet; I woke up. I kept the dream to myself. One week later my friend who was staying in my home had the same dream.*

What is a soulful, sacred space? Do we have to travel far and wide to go to one? To be sacred, does someone have to "Feng shui" it? Can the office be a sacred space? The mall? The gym? The freeway? The bathroom? What about the area where we put our trash?

Perhaps we should be asking ourselves a different question: What *is not* sacred?

Everything in creation derives from the Divine Source. When we recognize this, we see that even the lowliest bodily function is holy and should be treated with respect. If something is sacred to you, remember that it might not carry the same weight for another person.

There is one universal exception: Life is sacred. Adam, the ancestor of all human beings, was created from the dust of all four corners of the earth. Why? In order to instill in each of us that, despite our differences, we derive from the same Divine source.

## Reclaiming Space

I once was hired to read the energy of a house that had been sitting on the market for two years. I predicted that it would sell in nine days if the clients followed my suggestions. Busy Hollywood actors, the couple had a blended range of children who would all compete for attention. The marriage had a lot of strife, which was reflected in their home. By the time they consulted me, the behavior had reached to such a point that it was time for everyone to *literally* clean up his or her act!

First, I initiated a game of giving back for their children. They invested in their own growth by cleaning and completing chores; nothing is a better reality check than taking out your garbage and scrubbing your own floors! Cleaning up energy became a game for everyone, and sounds of laughter could be heard throughout the home. In addition to de-cluttering, I had them plant flowers together in their garden (a task usually reserved for gardeners). These simple moments of joy, of giving to the Earth, made them feel secure enough to calm down for a few moments. The kids began to take on some responsibility, which opened up hearts and smiles. Nine days after Coach Tyger gave Team Hollywood a kick in the rear, a buyer came and the house was sold. So much for the fortune spent on fancy staging!

Giving is one of the most attractive actions any one of us can use in any moment. Further, it is essential: we must give to receive. When we put aside our egos and work as a team, anything is possible.

**Tibet in Southern California**

I first met K shortly after he arrived in the United States from Kumbum, the oldest monastery in Tibet. K was in Los Angeles to attend UCLA on scholarship, where he later became the first Tibetan monk to receive a PhD in Public Health. He was giving a lecture on meditation at the house of another of Master X's students. I brought some friends with me and we listened while K spoke earnestly in broken English of the harsh conditions in Tibet. When he was finished, I was so moved by his speech, I decided to become involved with his newly formed nonprofit for Tibetan women and children.

Over the next few years, K stayed in my home with me when he was on break from his studies. Although I was then a vegetarian, at his request, I cooked whole chickens, which he gobbled with relish. (Most people do not realize that Tibetan monks who did not grow up in India eat meat. Their land is rocky and, due to the altitude, it is not easy to grow crops). As K says, they are grateful to have food—period—and will eat what is put in front of them. But, boy, did K like my chicken!

K was funny and cranky at the same time, and he shared what he knew about Buddhism, which was significant. At age five, he had begun training at the monastery where the Dalai Lama himself was schooled. So the lessons were very authentic. While I liked the practice of meditation, and learned valuable information from both Master X and K, our philosophies and approaches to life were fundamentally different. Still, for the next ten years I was an advisor and major fundraiser for the organization K founded. I was also the main clairvoyant of the North American chapter of Master X's meditation school. K's organization built the first pre- and postnatal clinic in Tibet where care was given to patients in their native language.

In return for my assistance, I was given sacred art, called Tsongas, from Tibetan monks and nuns. The Tsongas were made out of silk and depicted paintings of their deities, some as large as three-by-five feet. My house looked like a Buddhist monastery, and had the energy of one, akin to someone who had taken a vow of poverty and celibacy and surrounded themselves with graven images. But I was in a fog and did not realize what was truly happening.

I knew the paintings were given out of gratitude, so I felt it would be okay to display them. However, some gifts, even given with the best intentions, might oppose needs of your soul. Once, I was lying under a Tsonga, when I heard soft whispers saying, "Deception, deception," seemingly from the gold threads ingrained in the green silk. At first I thought I was dreaming, but then I heard it again. Initially, it led me to uncover a particular situation with someone who indeed was acting deceitfully. There are many levels of truth and, much later, I realized the Tsonga was also revealing its illusory nature.

It is important for people understand that decorating a house like a Tibetan monastery does not make you enlightened. Monks and nuns surround themselves with images and objects that will help them keep them to their vows of poverty and celibacy, which is incongruent with western households. Desires for material and personal gain are not in accordance with this philosophy. If we had the eyes to see and the ears to hear, we would know that even an idol, made from human hands, is forced to reveal its nature in the presence of the Holy Name, which is in all things.

## Creating a Soulful Space

Every one of our deeds, no matter how seemingly insignificant, is key to the welfare of our planet. Individually, we can help restore balance and equanimity, or the opposite. Every moment is a choice.

Setting intention in our own personal environments begins in the mind and ends with our actions. People who are spiritually bankrupt may live in a palace, but will never find happiness in their surroundings. Many people dissatisfied with their surroundings put their faith in blind application of vague Feng shui solutions. They adopt the mindset that that if they put that fountain in the corner, buy that talisman, or place that crystal just so, that their bank account will swell and they will find that perfect mate, take off ten pounds, or even develop six-pack abs! It is harder to look where *we* are responsible for our situations. When we work on peace within ourselves, this in turn attracts positive energy, which will always impact our environment. Sometimes we just have to be patient. Simple, benevolent acts can align us to infinite possibilities, including miracles.

Whether you intend to make money in your business or to create a peaceful space to live in, inspiration begins with a thought that is fueled by an emotion and carried out by the will. Do not give up if you have not seen your intentions manifested to fruition; this is a blessing, as it means there is a greater plan designed for you.

**Tyger Tip: Moving the Worm**

The universe has a code. As you become connected to higher plains of consciousness, you grow more aware of this code and the interconnectedness of all things. You can move your own destiny by any act of benevolence.

For example, if you are walking and a worm in peril catches your attention, if you can assist it without harming yourself, do so, be practical. Acts of compassion alter the energy around an individual, no matter how seemingly small, we are all connected as a unified whole in the fabric of time and space. Who knows what kind of positive ripple effect this outwardly insignificant good deed has had on your future?

## Mindfulness

I live by a nature preserve, and when the seasons change, spiders like to come into my apartment for warmth or to cool down. My policy is to find a cup and a piece of paper to capture and release outside. It never fails: no matter how far away, the minute I locate the spider, it senses my thought and quickly moves to hide. Many creatures, including plants, have an innate sixth sense and an intelligence that allows them to communicate their desires or needs. If a spider can sense intentions, surely a human being can too.

It is important to frequently question our perception of any given situation. Kabbalah speaks of worlds within worlds that exist alongside us. The Sages tell us that, should we learn to perceive these places, we could quickly lose our hold on reality. So it is not important that we actually see them, but to know about their existence. This teaches us to be less ridged in our thinking.

## Mysterious Messages from the Elements

Individuals who are highly sensitive to energy and have accessed their intuitive abilities can pick up on hidden messages. There are countless mysteries we have yet to resolve, and even more uncharted. Over 95 percent of the ocean remains unexplored. The following is the first and only time I picked up a message from water.

A friend of mine brought me salt from Hawaii. It had been excavated from 2,200 feet beneath the oceans' surface and was completely untouched by humanity. Excited to make use of this gift, I poured the crystal white mineral in the bath and filled it with water. When I immersed myself in the tub, my body felt like a needle on a record player, especially when I submerged the back and sides of my head (the energy centers for clairaudience). Within moments, I received an echoing message through my abilities. Here is some of it, from memory:

> *We come from the blue world that lives within yours.*
> *We come from the source that sustains all worlds.*
> *Man is destroying our world.*
> *We come from the world, which comes from the Word. Blessed is the Source of all worlds, who heals us.*

I was humbled and astonished. Here was water echoing the source from which it sprung. Unfortunately, I knew it would be hard to translate this moment in its entirety to others; so I kept the story mostly to myself.

Over four years later, I glimpsed into a mysterious world of snow. I was walking along a trail in Tyger Mountain, renewed from a recent blood transfusion after my N.D.E. and celebrating my rebirth. From the frozen lake next to the trail, I saw a blue orb dart between the trees. It appeared, whooshing back and forth in front of my eyes. I tried to follow it, but the light was moving too quickly—all I could do was watch. For this brief time, the veil between dimensions lifted and I peered into another world.

## Learning to Be Fluid

The Divine Architect designed the universe with curves and irregular shapes. Think about it—are there any straight lines in our bodies, in nature? Even the horizon has a curve to it. Only manmade objects and spaces have consistent straight edges. How did this come about? I believe it is because we have an inherent fear of being exposed. Most of us generally feel uncomfortable in a wide-open space with nothing around, no trees or mountains or even skyscrapers. We will want to create a boundary; something through which we can feel protected and can make sense of our existence in space. On a deeper level, many people have a hard time accepting divinity as a pervasive energy. The need to quantify everything makes it challenging for some to reconcile divinity, which has no boundary.

This need for boarders saturates our society, and can be felt in all realms, from social organization to business, learning, technology, and especially architecture. It costs less to use straight lines when building and designing. This has led us to adapt to living and working in boxes.

**Tyger Tip: Applied Mindfulness**

Let's examine our living spaces: In your personal living space, take a look and observe how many objects within are curved versus objects with straight edges. How much of what you live or work with reflects the curves of our natural world? This restricts our creative and learning abilities and changes how we think and perceive reality.

Thankfully, there are still individuals who break out of the box. A few genius architects dream higher and have created buildings with movement, like the Guggenheim Museum. If you have been lucky enough to visit one of these public spaces, you might have noticed that you felt differently when in the space or looking at it. These spaces help to expand our cognitive perception, which in turn, boosts our intuitive abilities and brainpower.

Though most of us are not architects, and tend to have smaller budgets to boot, you can still begin to round out sharp corners in your home by substituting straight-edged furniture or decorations with curvy items when possible. This has a calming effect on the nervous system and it can enhance creative thinking.

Whatever is before our eyes, intentionally or otherwise, influences us. Should we see great suffering and be unmoved, something is very wrong with the health of our soul. Evil dictators and those that carry out their will are an extreme example of this condition. They have fractured—and in some cases severed—their spirit from their consciousness, leaving them open channels for evil to penetrate further. We live in times where suffering is right before our eyes through social media. For the sake of your spirit, do not let yourself become impervious. Do not be afraid to cry to others about suffering that you see; it will spark the flame of their consciousness within them. If you work in the entertainment industry, be brave and take a stand against promoting unnecessary violence in media. This will help prevent our society from collective numbness.

## Tyger Teachings: Aromatherapy

Relaxation can facilitate mindfulness of our higher purpose. To that end, aromatherapy oils and flower essences work wonders. The olfactory sense essential to every aspect of healing and holistic health signals our brains to do all kinds of things—whether stimulating or calming!

Nostradamus, medieval French apothecary, physician, and seer, was very effective at treating his patients during the plague. He introduced hygienic measures like opening the windows to bring in fresh air and remove airborne bacteria. His aromatherapy practices, including with his famous "rose pill," which contained large amounts of vitamin C, all contributed to his success. I believe if modern hospitals reintroduced these practices, it could potentially aid in healing and recovery.

Plants and flowers work well in relaxing the senses, and they offer the added benefit of assisting with activating intuition. These essences can purify the outer layers of both the aura and the environment. As explained previously, the soul contains a pure inner light that will not tarnish unless we act self-destructively. I have found that prayer, immersion in water, and positive actions are simple, effective preventative steps. Aromatherapy dovetails easily with each. Essences might be used in a bath or diffuser, or breathed in using a tissue or bowl of steaming water.

A note to travelers: On the day of a trip, I recommend reciting *Tefilat HaDerech* (called the wayfarer's prayer in the English translation) or whatever prayer you are most comfortable with. Also, give to charity for mercy and protection. Additionally, I have found it useful to carry some soothing essences.

- *Lavender oil:* Calming, purifying; purple and deep blue, used for relaxation and expansion of intuition, to reduce stress
- *Rosemary:* Activating, purifying; good for awakening and strengthening the mind, with a reddish-gold energetic color; because it is so stimulating sensitive, people need to be mindful and use it only in minute amounts, preferably in a diffuser (never directly on the skin)
- *Lavender and rosemary combined:* Mixed together, they make an excellent remedy for sluggishness
- *Rose:* Uplifting, cleansing, with energetic colors of gold and orange-pink; it is wonderful to spray or otherwise scent bedrooms and living rooms to help create an attracting and joyful atmosphere
- *Honey:* The essence of honey sweetens and calms our environment; its color depends on its flowers or fruits: amber, violet, gold, and blue
- *Lemon:* Cleansing, uplifting moods
- *Jasmine:* Softens and connects to the feminine essence, a deeply intuitive scent with energetic colors of white and bluish violet
- *Yarrow:* Used for centuries in traditional herbal medicine to treat a variety of ailments, the golden

variety may be used occasionally as an external spray to help cope with environmental sensitivities; the effects are temporary and subtle

## Tyger Teaching: Soulful Spaces

I am well known in my circles for creating spaces that relax people. The books, paintings, and other objects in my living room are mystical and soul-oriented in nature. It is not unusual for my visitors to become so relaxed that they even become sleepy. Here are some of my tips for designing a soothing environment.

- *Lift the ceiling from your worries:* Regardless of your *age, place glow-in-the-dark stars on the ceiling in your bedroom. This simple change can help expand your consciousness from the mundane to the vastness of space and its infinite possibilities. Let the stars be a reminder of the Source from which you came, and where anything is possible.*

- *Instill tranquility, healing, flow, and intuitive abilities:* Decorate with green, aquamarine, blues, and purples, white, silver, and small amounts of gold.

- *Feel centered and grounded:* Earth tones and neutrals in living spaces are good for balancing opposing personalities living under one roof.

- *Give yourself a good night's sleep:* Do not store anything under the bed. And if you can, and it makes sense in the room, try facing the bed so the crown of your head faces east. It is preferable to use a wooden bed frame instead of metal or glass. Metal is mineral, a conductor of energy, so over time it can make sensitive people feel jittery or spacy. Similarly, glass relates to the element of air, which is freeing but offers no defined boundaries of time and space.

- *Support your productivity:* For the same reasons, it is easier to be productive working at a desk made from wood then one with a glass surface. Books and objects also hold and carry energetic imprints, which—depending on the content or origin—can, inspire, agitate, or arouse if you are sensitive to vibration.
- *Tend to your plant:* Plants can indicate how energy is flowing through your inner world and outer environment. When we neglect their care, it reflects some aspect of ourselves that is not being nurtured as well.
- *Avoid crystals indoors:* Crystals are best suited outside, where their mineral content can enhance the soil and beautify the garden. Some esoteric rituals recommend placing crystals in homes and business as talismans for purposes ranging from protection to enhancing an individual's prosperity or attracting a soul mate. However, I do not recommend keeping crystals indoors for several reasons. While I was in the ashram I was asked by the guru, students and clients to look at the energy of their crystals. In every case, over many years, I found that most crystals, like plants, emit and absorb energy at a low frequency, but unlike plants, it is energy that is meant to be underground. So placing them in bedrooms may agitate the elderly, children, and sensitive people. Especially if there is more than one, amplifying the magnetic frequency. (Do you really want your four-year old up more than usual? Probably not.)

**Mezuzah**

Many people who come to visit ask about the cylindrical metal cases on the right side of my doorways. I explain it is the *Mezuzah*, an ancient Jewish ritual of mindfulness. The mezuzah contains parchment inscribed with the first two lines of an ancient Judaic prayer, the Shema, declaring the oneness of creation and the Supreme Being. Encased in metal, thick plastic, or wood and placed inside the right side of a doorway to be easily seen upon entering or exiting. The mezuzah is a manifesto, a declaration of intention. It serves as a reminder to behave in conscious manner of love towards oneself and others, not only in our homes, but also as we go about our business in the world. In addition, it is a reminder of the Eternal One's omnipresence. On its cover is the letter, Shin, from the Hebrew alphabet, which represents one of the names of the Omnipotent signifying "guardian" (known as the name written with the three letters: shin, dale, and bud).

I have personally experienced, and seen in others, a difference in energy and mindfulness in the spaces where *mezzo* (plural of mezuzah) are present. I do not believe that one has to be Jewish to practice this concept; it benefits all of humanity. Doors notoriously make you forget things. If you are on an errand and walk through a doorway, it is very likely you will forget why you came. Imagine if every structure had a symbol on the door—whether a workplace, home, or school—that would remind you of the Creator's constant presence. Having a symbol on the door like a mezuzah can help remind you of why you are here in the world. This will put things into perspective and will help uplift your self-esteem.

Each of the six directions, including up and down, contain specific energy. Detailing their properties alone could fill up a whole book, but for this one all you need to know is that facing east helps with focus, concentration, and relaxation (which is why many traditions, including Judaism, call to face east when praying). Most importantly, acts of *chassed* (kindness and good deeds) supersede superstitions regarding negative directions.

Intentionally creating a sacred environment to live or work in can help elevate your psyche. However, if you find yourself operating from an angry, dissatisfied, or depressed place (we are only human), your own negativity may influence your environment, regardless of what is in it. This is why your most important safeguard to tranquility and sanctity lies, not in external objects, but within yourself. Life is the Holiest thing. That means you, so respect it, and yourself!

**Ignoring the Intuitive Stoplight**
During my time working with the Tibetans, I trained with Grand Master X, a Pilipino with Chinese ancestry. A beautiful human being who did much to help others, he had gained a following of almost a million students worldwide. Nevertheless, he took me under his wing. After a few years of intensive study under his guide, I became a medical intuitive.

This new profession made a heavy impact on my ability to help others, but it came at an enormous sacrifice to my welfare. I could not live a normal life. I decided to move to Ojai, an artist's community about eighty miles drive up the coast, in order to leave the "noise". North of L.A., Ojai was known for its healers and mystics. I had always felt strangely drawn to the valley, and initially felt right at home. But that was on a day pass—becoming a resident was a whole other pot of crazy . . .

At the time, people lived in all kinds of situations in Ojai. From Yurts and campers to multimillion-dollar ranches, there was something for everyone. Before we moved there, my boyfriend and I frequented a bed and breakfast. We came so often, that when the owners built a long-term residence behind the hotel; they reserved the top floor for us. It had a private sundeck on the roof in the shape of a tower, 2,000 square feet, hardwood floors, and double Jacuzzis. Fully furnished in rich tapestries, it was simply stunning. But this being Ojai, things were never as they seemed. When it was first built, the building was zoned for a bed and breakfast. Only one apartment was allowed to have a stove. (Not ours, of course, so we eventually lived in this *gorgeous* penthouse . . . with a hot plate.) Before we could even move in, our personal Taj Mahal had to be completed. So we rented a house in a rural part of the valley. The place had twenty-two trees and was set across from an abandoned cluster of old buildings. Not good energy alignment. I felt uneasy; my clairvoyant "antenna" was going off.

When I asked my future landlord what was up with the adjacent property, she told me twenty-five years ago it had once been a nursing home. She claimed it had become derelict due to a lack of developers. I ignored my intuition, which was raising plenty of red flags, and instead decided to ask the oracle in Tibet for a reading. The predictions came back that everything would be fine . . . which I guess in the long run it was.

Ignoring my inner compass, I went ahead and rented the house, rationalizing that it was just a short time until my apartment would be ready. (Thank G-d I put *mezuzahs* on the door; they protected us from what was to come.) The first night we were in the house, black widows crawled out from the cracks in the walls. So many came, you could hear them as they ran across the floor. Apparently, the landlord did not believe in pest control. We spent the rest of the evening sleeping with the light on. The next day, Joseph went to work, leaving me alone. I decided to meditate on the bench outside that was between two trees. After a few chants and some breathing exercises, I went inside the house. About ten minutes later, I looked out the window and thought: funny, I do not remember seeing an adobe-colored garden hose. Then I saw the 'hose' curl up and slither under the bench. It was the biggest snake I had ever seen, well over six feet. I am not generally afraid of them, they are to Southern California what bears are to the Northwest, but I never saw anything that looked like that before. Of course I screamed, but there was no one to hear me. I must have scared it, as I watched it slither off into a pile of rocks on the land.

After about an hour or so, I summoned the courage to go outside and find a neighbor. As I walked out the gate of the property I saw a couple of vultures swoop down, looking for prey. Initially I always look for non-esoteric meaning when strange things happen, a skill developed in reaction to watching too many students jump to conclusions around the guru. To them, everything was supernatural. I tried to keep my feet on the ground. So I started reasoning: *Well, this is a rural place*, and *I have seen vultures flying around when I am driving up the roads on a hot day.*

Over the next couple of days, our front yard was their freeway. A few days later, after falling asleep with the light on, I saw an apparition hover at the foot of the bed. It appeared to be a woman whose face was set against twisted green leaves. She wore a gown composed of rocks and shrubs. Peering out of the folds were pigs with contorted faces. My heart began to beat faster and my mouth became dry. Joseph was asleep next to me, but I could not find my voice to wake him. The creature informed me that she was the queen of the place, and how dare I, a human, set foot on her land? I was stunned. Somehow I began to whisper the holy words from the ancient prayer, Shema, over and over, my voice growing stronger each time. The creature disappeared. I woke Joseph and told him we would be leaving.

However, morning came and, that day, the landlady decided to send a worker over to fix the roof. The burly man arrived, bearded and in his fifties, with tattoos and a strange aura. After he introduced himself, he removed his shirt. Though it was hot, well over 90 degrees, this was too much. I stood clutching my cell phone outside. I did not want to go inside and find any more surprises. After twenty minutes, he came down from the roof and asked for some water. Taking a sip, he looked across the road and started grinning. He told me he spent time there in his youth. It had been a minimum-security prison and had "made a man out of him." Due to the rural area, the prisoners slaughtered pigs and chickens onsite as part of the work program. Twenty-five years later, the surrounding energy was still damaged and in need of repair.

Lesson learned: Unless you are willing to add more chaos to the mix when you are looking for a place to buy or rent, if it makes alarm bells go off in the inside, listen to your intuition. **Walk away!**

CHAPTER SIX

# Intuitive Listening

*I swam to the pier in the early morning of night, and then climbed up onto the dock. A showerhead was suspended in midair. After I rinsed off, I took a few steps and fell through space—a soul without a body. I flew over roads surrounded by lush green trees smoking with white fire. Then I reached a synagogue and joined the people inside. We lay with our bodies and faces prone on the floor, praying as the* shofar *was blown. Suddenly my body materialized and became one with my soul. I stood up and was ready.*

Listen carefully. Patterns are imprinted in a person's voice. The voice is an instrument that our soul uses to communicate with others. History has revealed how leaders, both good and bad, can influence others through the power of their speaking voice. Why? A person's voice is as unique as a fingerprint. There are specific imprints in vocal patterns that translate through sound as wave patterns, called voice biometrics. These waves can pull us in hypnotically or repel us, like any sound.

Our good and our bad inclinations can be heard through our voice. Depending on which inclination society is following, we will follow suit. Entire movements are born from speech, whether from a politician, dictator, or spiritual leader. These movements are created from the speakers' ability to connect to their audience. Now more than ever, we need to notice the messages that surround us and apply intuitive listening to determine their essence.

You will find that the more you develop your intuition, the more sensitive you will become to sound. Music is a key part of my everyday life. I create a soothing, elevated environment at home: I play classical music from morning until evening, interspersed with songs of prayer. This is not just for myself, but also for my plants, which thrive with such music. Sound is everywhere, though it is important to listen to natural sounds rather than mechanical ones. The composition of sound involves patterns of waves and vibrations that are carried through the natural four elements. Sitting in an auditorium while an orchestra is playing is far different from listening to a radio or computer. While I could play music through speakers at work, I prefer to play an instrument to make the vibration physically present, even just momentarily.

**Listening to Your Inner Voice**

When we first met, Joseph and I lived in different worlds. He was a model who posed for magazine covers and underwear ads. While he lifted weights, I read people's futures and chanted mantras. We were clichés, and were each extreme in our respective approach to life. At that time in our lives, being together balanced us out and made us better people, a perfect illustration of how opposing natures can come together for collective well-being. The following is an example of how we both used intuitive listening to affect reality.

One day, I decided to take a break from work and drive up the coast to a secluded beach. About twenty miles into my jaunt, I felt a strong voice in my head urging, *Go home!* Having made a terrible mistake in the past by ignoring a similar premonition, I turned around. The voice became stronger and more repetitive, until it stopped within a five minutes' drive from my house.

As I paused at a stoplight, I looked to my left and saw half a dozen dogs fleeing a recently opened animal care center. The animals were running in between six lanes on Washington Boulevard. Cars were braking and swerving in order not to hit the dogs or each other. It was chaotic and extremely dangerous.

I made it to my driveway, exited my car, and ran inside. Joseph was home and I asked him to follow me immediately. Without question, he dropped what he was doing and we ran to the doggie daycare center. (Later, he admitted that his intuition has been nagging him about some vague danger). The door was open. A man was standing in shock, holding a broom, with blood running down his leg. Dogs were everywhere. In the corner, a pit bull had latched its teeth onto a puppy's neck that was howling in pain.

In one swift move, Joseph grabbed the pit bull by the back of its neck, and tore it off the puppy. Then he secured the pit bull in an adjacent empty room, slamming the door, until someone could safely deal with the manic dog. After checking that the man with the broom was okay, we picked up the injured puppy and rushed it to the vet. By this time, other people had come in from the street to help. Later that day, we found out the owner had gone on vacation and left a rookie in charge. Though I "heard" the cry for help twenty miles away, there was no way I could have done anything without X's physicality—his animal instincts allowed him to intuitively and courageously protect multiple futures and lives. No matter how clairvoyant or spiritual we are, it is only by integrating these gifts with physical action that we are truly effective.

**The Tyger Technique for Intuitive Listening**
Applying my techniques of intuitive listening to a conversation allows you to better hear hidden cues in speech. This will lead to greater interpersonal skills. When somebody speaks, listen carefully and see if you can detect their voice's source of power and discern which energy center their voice most closely aligns with. For example:

- When a person speaks from the heart, you will hear the compassion in their tones. Their words will comfort and uplift your being, and you will be energized in the speaker's presence.
- A person who is cerebral and also enthusiastic can instill greater focus in listeners. Without the enthusiasm, the speaker's message will seem dry and overly analytical and will not hold the audience's attention.
- Self-serving people will speak from their instinctual nature. If you pay attention, narcissists can be identified by tones of entitlement and anger.
- When a person is overtly sexual, they oftentimes have issues with power and can speak hypnotically; their voice deepens, seemingly coming from their lower torso where the sex chakra is spinning.

**Tyger Tip: What is Your Response?**
As you listen to others, be mindful of how you react to a person's voice and what part of your energy centers it affects. In a dating situation, if you have feelings of an-

ger, doubt, hostility, and repulsion from the get-go, take notice and move on. If you are immediately attracted to someone's voice, be cognizant, as it means they can have a strong influence on you. Discern whether or not this is positive.

Similarly, pay attention to how you respond to magnetic and charismatic world leaders. To understand where they are speaking from, take note of what part of your body seems to be affected by their voices. If a voice affects your heart center, it indicates compassion, and the person's influence will almost certainly be positive. Does a voice zap your adrenaline? Does it activate laughter or aggression? Charismatic people often trigger extreme reaction on both sides of the spectrum.

When you are having trouble judging someone favorably, try this exercise to deactivate your negative response: We know we cannot do anything to change his or her behavior. However, if train our minds to remain neutral, we can stay present with the individual. You will hear what they are actually saying and not your opinions and perception of their words. To this end, I recommend turning down the dial and slowing down. Calm the body, stand still, and speak slower and more evenly. Take a moment and think, not react. Kabbalah teaches that words give fuel to anger. So best thing to diffuse unfavorable opinions like anger or harsh judgment is to remain silent, even for the span of thirty seconds.

The best gift you can give yourself and the world is to integrate your heart and engage your mind. When that is achieved, you realize that everything has a shelf life. That which is in front of you today might not be there tomorrow. You will become more mindful of being in the moment, and more likely to notice that you have never *really* been stuck in any situation (even if sometimes it feels like it). You can move through any terrain if you remain committed to your destination. By maintaining this mindfulness, you will have an easier time accepting the present. When change comes, as it always does, you will be prepared for the challenge.

In our modern, noisy world, where most people are numb to the sheer volume that surrounded us, it can feel more like a curse to be sensitive to sound. Our offices, schools, and hospitals are constantly humming with generators, computers, lights, and so on. I am sure, with our evolving technology, we have the means to work on more pleasing auditory environments, but it has not been made a priority by engineers. I believe that when society does so, we will reduce the current consumption of medication for stress disorders. As we become more cognizant of sounds around us, we will also become more aware of our nervous systems and how they are affected. So, advocate taking things down a notch where you can. Your auditory, nervous, lymphatic, and endocrine system will thank you.

## Your Pineal Gland

If reducing stress, anxiety-related medications, and generally soothing your body systems does not motivate you, the following might: reducing noise pollution and increasing meditation and prayer opens and activates the pineal gland. In other words, it helps to produce anti-aging hormones! That's right, a quieter environment is healing *and* beautifying—and it activates intuition!

Located in the center of the brain, the pineal gland, an endocrine gland sometimes called the "master" gland, also produces the hormones responsible for our moods, sleep patterns, and reproductive ability. The medical community used to commonly believe that as we age, the pineal gland loses its ability to function and effectively produce melatonin and serotonin. Reduced amounts of these "happy hormones" can lead to all kinds of problems, such as insomnia, weight gain, depression, agitation, and even loss of youthful appearance. However, science is now finding what mystics have long known about the positive effects meditation, prayer, and sound on the pineal gland: In esoteric and schools of eastern healing modalities, the pineal gland is referred to as the third eye. From personal experience, I can verify that the above combination can make a person feel happier, sleep better, and look (some say) years younger. Certainly more invigorated!

**Master Gland, Wake Up!**
For the next week, pay attention to all the sounds in your environment. Tune in and turn down your television, stereo, iPhone, etc.—just one notch. Consider offering suggestions at work on ways to create a better auditory experience for yourself, for clients, especially for patients! If you work in fashion or hospitality, consider taking the initiative to encourage the decision makers to cycle in some classical music. Or at least turn down the endless thumping a notch or two. I promise you, long-term exposure to this type of noise helps no one. No matter what the age! Nor does it drive sales. It simply makes a person numb, angry, over stimulated, and unproductive.

Billions of neurons in the brain generate electrical impulses that emit frequencies or waves that stimulate our thoughts and behavior. The most commonly known are alpha, beta, delta, gamma, and theta. There is fascinating science behind this that is beyond the scope of this book, but I encourage you to go out and explore further if you are interested.

## The *Shofar*, the Sound of Awakening

The *shofar* is an ancient wind instrument fashioned from a ram's horn. Traditionally blown at the start of the Jewish New Year on Rosh Hashanah ('Head of the Year' in English), it is used spiritually as a wake-up call to the soul. According to Kabbalah, the sounds of the shofar are believed to purify and dispel negativity from those who hear it. What better way to commence a new year than with a blast of such ancient, powerful sounds! The shofar is blasted over one hundred times during the synagogue service, and by the time it has finished I feel as exhilarated and charged as if I was walking in the forest in the rain. It cleanses a person of negative thoughts and emotions; I can personally attest to seeing gold light surrounding the horn-blower and spilling out into the space. Recently, I watched a video of a mystic from Safed blowing a *shofar* while attached to a device that claims to measure auras. One could clearly see what appeared to be whitish-violet light surrounding the player's head and shoulders. Exactly in the same areas I have seen myself.

During the New Year, my friend will blow the shofar in my apartment. (Talk about space clearing!) We usually have guests over, and the sensitive ones report to feeling a buzzing sensation on their foreheads and encircling their heads, pointing to the exact spots that various healing modalities identify as energetic pathways to higher consciousness. These same spots are also where *Tefillin*, an ancient Kabbalistic practice, are placed to activate spiritual awakening.

Sounds and music are universal, and they can help bridge the gap between individuals to bring us closer to each other, regardless of our differences. One day, the shofar may be blown to announce peace between all nations.

## Sound, Vibration, and Intuition

Clairvoyance and even intuition is about seeing or hearing the future. Typically, these senses can bombard you and force you into a constant attempt at balance. The ultimate aim is functionality in the world.

For clairaudients or those in an altered state, music can create a mystical experience by forming images within the mind's eye. Be mindful of the type of music, as cacophonous sounds can create disharmonious experiences. I prefer classical music, as the inspiring sounds and colors lift my spirit. My aura opens and relaxes. When I attended a concert in Benaroya Hall of master violinist, Yitzhak Perlman. Seated close to the stage, my eyes closed, I felt a familiar whirling vibration accompanied by a faint buzz on the top of my head and in the space between my eyebrows. Intrinsically, I was mindful the clairaudient was activated.

Can one remain in this state for very long? No. Such a thing is impossible until we shed our bodies. Still, when we meditate or pray with our hearts, in that moment, we touch infinite intelligence. High-vibration sounds help us to connect to infinite consciousness, where time appears to stand still.

That evening in Benaroya Hall, I allowed myself to drift into a place where I was unaware of time. The sensation took and floated with the music. When I was younger, training with the guru, I was unable to control this ability. Now I can direct my clairaudient and clairvoyant nature to enjoy concerts psychically without reading the next day's headlines. You can too, as well, should you possess these abilities as you learn to focus.

## Train Your Ear

Meditation calms the brain waves in your head. Similarly, focusing can help tune out unwanted noise. How relaxed would you feel if you were listening to rainfall or a gentle stream? Can you recreate this feeling at home? At the doctor's office? At work? What do you need to do for a healthier auditory environment?

The main hub of productivity is the work environment, a place where you often lack control over the sounds of electromagnetic fields. Even so, you should *still* adjust your auditory environment, if possible, with classical or soft music. To further make it a relaxing space, consider the overall frequency of your workspace: are the colors right? Do you need some plant life? Working in a calm manner is conducive to success. Cerebral work such as studying, using computers, creating, cooking, and so on, requires an environment that facilitates focus, which in turn ups your productivity. With practice, you will eventually learn to tune out noises, which will help develop your power to focus.

This is perhaps most important to consider when you are going to sleep. Start by turning off all electromagnetic fields at night: computers, modems, phones, televisions, and so on. Why leave them on? Turn them off and your nervous system will thank you.

**Tyger Tip: Change It Up**
Consider attending a classical music concert, ballet, visiting a school for the deaf, or even taking a workshop on animal communication. All of these activities involve the communication of a collective on an intuitive level. Surrounding yourself with these types of interaction will open your awareness and stimulate your brain, thereby heightening your intuitive skills.

**Exercise: Activating Intuitive Listening**
Intuitive listening can facilitate deeper communication, which in turn fosters more effective speaking. I have a friend who, at twenty-nine, is already known for his intellectual brilliance. One day, he will turn the world around with his theories. By his nature, though his mind whirls like a computer, he speaks very slowly. So much so, in the beginning of our relationship, I found it exasperating. For us to continue in friendship, I had to alter my expectations of the conversation. Rather than having a quick back and forth tennis match, we would play golf, so to speak. Over time, I learned to become a better listener by slowing down the timing of how I listened the expectations of verbal delivery. Becoming a better listener affected my speech, as I took greater care communicating with others and relating to people by being more present in any conversation.

Try this exercise to sharpen your intuitive listening skills: For the next seven days, practice listening deeply to a child or elderly person. Be present with them. Really listen, without filling quiet moments or imposing your own ideas.

Next, try someone who truly annoys you. Instead of rushing to the next "thing," intentionally encourage them to discuss the day's event, or another topic of interest. Initially, you might find yourself becoming impatient, irritated, or both. However, stay mindful that you are developing greater intuitive listening skills, which leads to powerful insight into the human condition we are all experiencing. When we developing greater communication skills, we will see people connecting to our words and our confidence and self-esteem will grow.

CHAPTER SEVEN

# The Importance of Dreams

*I had a dream my forehead and eyes were indigo, with dozens of flowers embedded on my shoulders; green leaves grew from my feet. A beautiful woman cleansed my hands while I prayed with her. The clairvoyance was different now, I just knew: sense, smell . . . No longer a ghost, I walked through the forest on solid ground, not afraid to see or fly anymore. I had come back for you— for the future—again . . .*

For several months in 2001, when I was in the meditation school, I had a recurring dream in which I was in a plane through New York City, flying between buildings. I would wake up in a sweat, reaching for X.

The first week of September arrived, and Joseph was due to fly to New York from Los Angeles for Fashion Week, to model in the shows for the first time. I had such a bad feeling about it that, though we could have really used the money, I asked him not to go. I hid his ID and refused to give it back to him. We argued, but I was adamant.

I was still using Tarot cards then, and though many of my clients were international, no matter who it was or where they called from, the same card would appear. I knew something dreadful was coming. It occurred to me that the feeling was somehow tied into my dream, but I dismissed the premonition, ascribing it to my dislike of flying.

Two weeks before 9/11, I had another dream, but it still did not connect the dots. On the night of September 10th, I felt such a sense of dread that I wrote an email to Grand Master X, who was teaching in India. This is the message I wrote:

**Monday, September 10, 2001 3:41 AM**
*Dear Grand Master X,*

*Two weeks ago I had a dream, here it is: I was in a place with fifteen hundred or two thousand people. It was the Jewish Holiday, Yom Kipper, and everyone was fasting. A white bird flying from above and behind was to meet them at the altar. I was told to look. I was able to fly over people's heads and see that the bird was intercepted midair and enclosed in a plastic bag and set on fire. The bird was in flames. Only a young, non-human woman and I could see this. She was crying. I was told that her tears could put out the fire, but a human had to save the bird. Her tears stopped the fire and I caught the bird that was dying . . . I could see its pink tongue. The young girl was weeping still and I tried to bring the bird to the masters to heal.*

*I woke up. It seems that this is the Middle East and it will take place around Yom Kipper, and that the young girl was pure, and not of this world. The attack will come from behind, where people least expect. Surely a mass meditation to send light to the area will help us all. It must come from humans.*

*Love and respect,*
*Tyger*

I did not put the two dreams together. But if I had, what could I have done? I did not have the complete picture. I woke Joseph up at 5:30 a.m. PST and told him I heard wolves howling. Two hours later, a friend called and told us to turn on the news.

May they be blessed forever; I have no answers.

Several hours later, I was in the emergency room (the first of many times to come, though they did not find anything this time) with pain with my colon.

We rid ourselves of our television, and I did not fly again for ten years.

## Dreams: the Unifying Thread

No matter the differences in cultures and religion throughout history, all agree that humanity dreams. This means, even a prisoner in a cell can be free on a mountain when he dreams. So much nonsense is set up in schools, for the next generation to memorize—useless facts and endless tests; but this basic gift, inherent in us all, is rarely explored or addressed. This is true despite the greatest thinkers, visionaries, leaders, mystics, and inventors often attributing their inspiration and successes from dreams. Many of Einstein's theories arose from daydreams and naps, which are *de rigueur* for a deeper relationship with one's soul. Although human potential is unlimited, it is Divine inspiration that makes potential a reality. Divine inspiration helps us to become infinite, so connecting with dreams is one of the best ways of connecting with the infinite.

What are dreams, anyway? How do we interpret them? What should we pay attention to and what should we dismiss? Interpreting our dreams can be a lifelong pursuit that unfolds in layers. Some dreams, especially when they are recurring, may take months or years to decode. But as someone who has experienced life-saving guidance from dreams, I know they can be used as a tool to understand our soul's journey through the world.

Dreams have been an integral part of my gift and my soul's journey. My most lucid dreams come during Shabbat and certain festivals. We know from the Kabbalah and physicists' research that time is not linear; the past, present, and future run together simultaneously. When we partake in a Sabbath, we rest with our Creator as in the beginning. Fridays are my favorite day; the energy of the Sabbath awaits me and, if I prepare properly, I may access certain dimensions that are not revealed during the rest of the week. For example, when we dream, though our body lies on the bed, we might be flying over mountains. This can seem as real as the experience of being awake. So where are we? Can we be in two spaces at once? Where do our minds go? Have you ever dreamt you saw yourself sleeping from somewhere else in the room? From above? In a darkened room?

While we are alive, a portion of our soul remains rooted in the upper world, as the higher soul. Depending on our level of consciousness, we can reconnect with this part of our soul when we dream. True righteous ones *(tzaddikim)* can go to these worlds when they sleep and study the ancient texts. Moreover, they can *retain* the knowledge when they wake.

But how receptive are we? Most of us do not even recollect our dreams. Partly because our consciousness is buried under the noise of our lifestyle, leaving us numb to the inner dialogue between our body and spirit. But whether you are male or female, everyone's nature is receptive to insight. To access our dreams and their intuitive messages, we have to calibrate our sensitivity.

**Exercise: Increase Mindfulness and Define Goals**

Build awareness with this exercise to become more mindful of where your time and energy is being spent.

Take paper and pen and draw a circle like a pie. First, think of the pie as your life, and divide it up into sections: appearance, acquiring tangible assets, family, creativity, marriage or partnership, sexuality, career or work, spirituality, volunteering, friendships, pets. Be as honest as possible and write down the percentage you spend developing or involved with each. You will be amazed when you see exactly where and with whom you spend most of your time. Then ask yourself, if you do nothing to adjust your current trajectory, what will your life look like in six months? One year? Will you be any closer to your goals or dreams being accomplished?

For instance, if you want to be married, have a child, or publish that book, will you have to sacrifice something else in order to achieve that future? Do not believe anyone who says you can have it all or manifest your dreams just by positive thinking. I have worked with enough multimillionaires, celebrities, and people from all walks of life to tell you it is simply not true. Success in life takes careful thought combined with focus, intention, action, and—most importantly—our connection with the Higher Power to access our true blessings. Oftentimes, what we want is not what is actually best for us.

Next, draw a circle of how things would look if the Internet, television, cell, and so on, were reduced by just 25 percent. In these new spaces, pencil in activities that do not include mass media. You have to think for a minute, right? Examine how much virtual reality has become your own. Our nervous systems and energy bodies are overloaded with technology, lessening our ability to create an internal world in the absence of external stimuli. Over time, our intuitive creative muscle becomes flabby and, eventually, paralyzed. Someone who unplugs even 25 percent more than the average person is going to have a greater advantage in life, reaping the benefits of enhanced focus, greater clarity, and a calmer spirit.

If we reduce the daily distractions that detract from our soul awareness, we will better understand the kind of dreams that can help fulfill our life's purpose. In other words, we must each familiarize ourselves with our own soul. This will allow us to develop an inner world, something essential for recognizing and discerning that which is truly important for inner growth. Excess pursuit of materialistic and superficial goals bankrupts the spirit, leaving you with nothing to draw from. Want meaningful dreams? Make it a point to create physically and spiritually meaningful experiences in your life.

Dreams can impart invaluable lessons to change our reality. But how can you tell if what you are dreaming is a message from your soul or the movie and soundtrack of what you have literally and figuratively consumed? For instance, a recurring dream, positive or negative, can present itself symbolically or in true-to-life images. Depending on the spiritual maturity, the soul can interact with its conscious nature. This comes from practicing respect for sanctity and compassion for others.

## Decoding Dreams

The following are some questions to ask to help you decipher if last night's dream, was a message from your soul rather than something you ate:

- *When you wake from the dream, does it stay with you?*
- *Does it come back to you during moments of stillness?* Intuition comes to us like a consistent whisper.
- *Does it motivate you to take action, even though you are not sure what that may be?* Intuition is a directive from the soul to the body, which likes to communicate through movement. When the soul is in charge, the will of the body orients towards positive actions.
- *Was it in color?* Intuition is part of the inner world, which is multicolored.
- *Did it come true?* If you can answer yes to any of these questions, then most likely your dream derived from your soul's guidance.

To better decipher the message, over the next several weeks, notice whether a common thread runs through your dreams. The best way to observe this is to keep a journal by your bed. Take note when reoccurring images appear in different scenarios; these symbols are codes from your intuition, foreshadowing a leap in personal growth, possibly requiring you to move away from a situation, or to return to one to make amends. For example, regular nightmares mean your soul is letting you know she is agitated by the actions of your body. (Think about what those might be; most likely you will not have to think long.) It is not our spirit that justifies and avoids, it is our instinctual drive, which for everyone has both a positive and negative aspects.

To interpret a dream requires sensitivity, experience, and patience to decipher messages from the soul. Certain symbols pertain to a collective experience; though it is filtered through our prism, each metaphor can hold a common meaning. For instance, dreaming of snow traditionally means purification and happiness within the soul. Other times, dreams take on particular patterns when certain conditions are happening in our lives, and these codes can be pertinent to the individual. For example, the purity interpretation might not make sense for a person who does not like snow. It is for the dreamer to understand themselves over time, sometimes over years.

That is why, ultimately, we must learn to define and decode the symbols within our dreams ourselves. However, while you familiarize yourself with the lay of your inner landscape, I have made a chart of some common symbols and their meanings.

**How to tell if you're having a Premonition Dream**
A premonition is where one has a sense, vision, or dream that foretells the future for a person, place, or thing. As we know, our futures can shift. So, if you have an uncomfortable dream that feels like a premonition, I recommend following the advice of ancient Kabbalistic sages:
- Repeat the phrase "I dreamt a good dream" aloud three times. It is always best to reinforce positive thoughts on any issue. The more you verbalize negative thought, the more you bring harmful energy into the world.

- There is an ancient Kabbalistic prayer, *Modeh Ani*, which is said upon waking. This prayer thanks the Creator for returning the soul back to the body. Traditionally, it is customary to follow the prayer with a ritual of washing the hands. Doing so cleanses the body of negative energy collected while traveling in the plane where dreams exist.
- Then make a donation to a worthwhile cause and go about your business in peace.
- Before you interpret the dream to others, try to put a positive light on it to further enhance the effectiveness of the above steps. This creates positive merit to awaken energies from the gates of Mercy, which is also stimulated when you touch water; both actions lessen energies of judgment that may have been revealed in your dream. If the dream is positive, the above steps are still helpful, as they will further accelerate its actualization into material reality.

One has to be as clear as possible in one's waking life to not confuse emotional disturbance with precognitive dreaming. Nightmares are, generally, not premonitions but a disturbance within your energetic field. True premonitions can be symbolic, which makes them not so easy to interpret.

Below is a case example that was clearly Divine guidance. Respecting its message ended up saving my life.

For years, though I had never seen the place, I felt I was supposed to live in Seattle. At the time, with my health being what it was, uprooting seemed ridiculous to my loved ones. But I intuited that the move would facilitate my healing. It was as if I had been implanted with an internal compass that pointed to the Pacific Northwest. One morning, I woke from a dream with the absolute certainty of premonition. Trusting the feeling completely, I went on the Internet to find a place to live—which I did, within moments. (That alone was something, considering what a struggle it had been anywhere else!) But after the initial euphoria and a few days had passed, I began to lose faith in my decision. I decided uprooting to a place I had never seen was too much, even for me. It was much better to put the whole thing out of my mind, and so I did. But a few nights later I went to sleep and dreamt that a map of the West Coast was in my hands. The state of Washington and the word, 'Seattle', were both bathed in golden light.

I caught the message.

Shortly after we arrived, the health problems that had plagued me for years were finally diagnosed correctly. During my recovery from the operation, I began to have a new dream. One in which I walked on a beach under a night sky filled with stars and then was engulfed by a huge wave of saltwater, yet I remained standing. I kept on walking until I reached a group of people seated at a long, white table. Their heads were covered and they were singing; silver candlesticks on the table were aglow with lighted candles. As I watched this, a white scarf fell from the sky to cover my head.

I had this dream for weeks until Rosh Hashanah, the Jewish New Year. I felt compelled to connect with my lineage, though I hardly knew anyone in Seattle and was not sure where to begin. My girlfriend on the East Coast found a Chabad synagogue near Tiger Mountain, where I like to walk and pray. So, I went there. Rebbetzin (rabbi's wife) Nechama greeted me at the door and smiled, beckoning me to enter. I recognized her instantly as one of the women seated at the table in my dream! I immediately felt comfortable and walked in. A few weeks later, she invited me to her home for Shabbat. As I walked into the dining room, I saw several people at a long white table set with gleaming silver candlesticks, singing songs for the Sabbath. This time, I joined them.

Sometimes, a message can hit home after just one dream. It might take more time for your soul to knock some sense into you, especially if you are stubborn, like me—which is why dreams recur!

## How to Improve Your Dreams

Most nightmares are caused by accumulated thoughts and images that we consume over a period of time. For highly sensitive people, just watching a few minutes of a scary film can cause a disturbance later. But preventing nightmares is not that complicated, in fact; it is so simple you might not believe me.

When we live healthier lives, our subconscious mind relaxes. If we want to have good dreams, we have to train the dream muscle metaphorically and figuratively. For example, what have your ears been listening to? Where have your eyes been looking? Whatever you have taken in during the day is going to be the movie and soundtrack when you sleep. I am not asking you to become a monk (who, by the way, have nightmares, too) but I am suggesting you approach sleep like anything else in your life that you want to become stronger: with respect.

The cumulative effect of sensory addiction has been to diagnosis everyone with attention-deficit disorder, depression, and whatever else. We do not know the long-term effects of medications that we freely give to our children and ourselves for these twenty-first-century afflictions. And yet, clearly, there is never a magic bullet—never one modality to cure what ails us. The human being is a complex system, and though the spirit cannot be measured, it must be addressed. One way of doing this is to allow us to dream in peace.

**Nighttime Attire**
Refrain from wearing the following colors to bed: orange, reds, dark browns, blacks, or any of the darker shades. Instead, aim for light colors and shades: whites, blues, turquoise, greens, and earthy shades. Purple is ok, but lighter shades are preferred. Yellow depends on the sensitivity of the individual, more analytical individuals should refrain from this color, as it activates their mind. Choose your clothing for bed accordingly. Fabrics should be very soft and breathable. Patterns are ok if they are calm or joyful. Better to avoid clothing with words, especially ones that you cannot translate.

**Rituals that Prepare Us to Enter the World of Dreams**
- Set a nightly curfew from as much external influence as you can: food, alcohol, drugs, television—even books! Scary, right? *Remember, it is you and your consumption that will be the movie and soundtrack when you sleep.* Give yourself at least thirty to sixty minutes to unwind before you enter the dream world. If you are really attached to falling asleep to the television, replace it with classical music from the radio. The voices from commercials can give you a fix while you wean yourself from listening to strangers'

voices to fall asleep. That's right: television should not be a lullaby that lulls you to sleep.

- Detach from the Internet—turn the modem off. Literally unplug for the night.

- Be sure that you do not keep or store things under your bed. Even inanimate objects have thought forms swirling around them, depending on what they are and to whom they belong. If you are sensitive, you may pick up on vibrations that may not be compatible with your personal imprint. The idea is to become free as possible of external "noise" (even if is just vibratory), when we lay down to rest.

- A step towards removing energy that binds us to our addictions is keeping our surroundings simple. For best rest, your house should be clean, with peaceful colors, and filled with life and sacred, meaningful books.

- Say a prayer for you to know and connect with your spiritual soul. Change it up every night; you can pray for the same thing but do not become redundant with your words. You will end up finding different parts of your prayer that will affect you differently.

- Imagine your prayer creating an opening in the Upper World, through which a ladder descends to you. Think about climbing the rungs and leaving your pressures and worries beneath you. As you climb, visualize the place of your dreams, whether it is an earthly destination or not. Visualize the landscape you would like to visit in your dreams and communicate with your soul, asking for guidance in the coming days.

- When you wake up in the morning, take a moment and thank the Creator for returning your soul to the body. Doing this helps to reinforce our connection with the Infinite, with something bigger than us. It brings us a cubic higher, which Kabbalah says is all we need to reach the space where miracles occur.

## Nourish the Soul for Sweeter Dreams

In addition to the emotional upheaval we already talked about, people can also have nightmares because their soul is not being nourished. When we live life just focused on the needs of the body, the soul feels ignored and will look for ways to let us know. If we continue to swim in unconsciousness, the soul becomes further agitated, and nightmares can be a byproduct.

A simple way to bridge this conflict is to acknowledge your soul before sleep. Remind yourself that your body contains a spirit, which allows the soul to escape from the daily chains of her suffocating existence in the body. When you create a space that lets your soul breathe, you will be enveloped in a sense of calm. Follow the steps above for finding peaceful sleep.

Additionally, I say the ancient Jewish prayer, The Shema, that I learned and been reciting since childhood. During my time in the ashram, no matter what I was chanting or meditating, at night before sleep, I returned to the Shema.

And connected . . .

Do this consistently for forty days. If practiced regularly, these rituals will reinforce your connection to Divine light and bring peace to your soul. The nightmares will stop or profoundly lessen.

For those individuals who never dream (or think you don't), either your instincts are on overdrive or your "dream muscles" are not strong enough to flex themselves or impress them on your consciousness. Either you are so bone tired from the day's events that you drop into a deep sleep and do not remember what you dreamt, you are on medication that does the same, or you are so numb from pain you are not connected to your heart. The remedies I have recommended throughout the book will help with all of this.

## Dream Dictionary

- *People who are wearing head coverings and/or close relatives:* Your soul is being comforted. Prepare for inner and outer transformation (though the effects can take up to ninety days to be revealed).
- *Birds:* Opportunities, the angelic kingdom, messengers.
- *Blue Birds:* There will be shift in your circumstances of revealed good
- *Fish:* Improved prosperity and abundance—the larger the fish greater the prosperity. If you see yourself feeding them, then with the Master Architect's blessings your income will begin to grow.
- *Bees:* If they are attacking you, beware of enemies; if they are peaceful, then industrious work coming your way.
- *Frogs:* If they are singing, rain is coming; if they are silent, perform prayer and charity to avert a possible Heavenly decree of drought.

- *Hawk:* Pay greater attention to your environment. Practice discernment in your dealings.
- *Heavenly Bodies or Stars:* You have strengthened the connection to your true purpose in life. Be patient; circumstances will begin to improve.
- *Dogs:* In Hebrew, the word *dog* means *like (the) heart,* which is very telling to the nature of this wonderful, inherently loyal animal. In a dream, different colors and locations may indicate true friendship or an enemy. If they are light to brown in hue, and in front of you or walking by your side, then you have attained honorable and true friendships. If they are dark and appear from behind, pay close attention to who and what you are engaging with, as it is not in your best interests.
- *Cats:* The hidden will be revealed.
- *Green trees:* New life, endeavors, fresh start, returning to your authentic self.
- *Silver:* Elevated vibrations and frequencies, gifts from Heaven. If wearing silver, then modesty and refinement.
- *Dragonfly:* Individually it signals transformation, especially of living conditions. In groups, a dramatic and significant shift in relationships.
- *Water:* If one is swimming peacefully in clear waters, prosperity, enhanced creativity, purification, especially if a wave washes over you that makes you happy. If, however, you are swimming in turbulent waters, the size of the waves will reveal the depth of the turmoil of the soul. Little waves, little discomfort; the larger the waves, the greater the agitation. (Should you be dreaming this type of scenario frequently I recommend

Psalm 15, 23 or 27 to help your soul be comforted. See chapter 7 for more on prayer.)

- *Snow:* Purity, inner forgiveness of your soul, happiness, joy, innocence beauty.
- *Fire:* The meaning depends on the size and distance from the dreamer. If close and small, it means disputes. If large, seen further away, and emits black smoke, it may be a forewarning of possible war (still preventable, if people collectively change their actions).
- *Earth:* If you see earth that it is rich and reddish in color, it may mean improved material circumstances. If muddy, or like quicksand, it may indicate lack of soul awareness or overt attachment to the mundane. (I recommend Psalm 27 or 30 in the morning and afternoon, and studying a few lines of sacred texts in the afternoon, for example, Ethics of the Fathers, *Pirkei Avot,* for forty days).
- *Flying:* Exploring the inner worlds and chambers of the soul, confidence.
- *Empty stage:* Unfulfilled ambitions, motivation, security, and insecurity, feeling disconnected from others, performing rather than experiencing or being.

## A Peek between Dimensions

I have undergone experiences where I have witnessed the duality of dimensions. The first time this happened, I was still in the meditation school. Ill with an unexplained condition, I went to bed early. I awoke and found myself standing outside my body, surprised to find it still asleep on the bed. Threads of light were emitting from my crown. Confused as to where I was or how this was happening, I looked around the room. Nothing seemed unchanged from how I had gone to sleep, except that light was peeking through the windows.

The next I knew, I woke up startled, back in my body. Daylight was peeking out of the window.

The next time I perceived this duality was years later when I was in the hospital. A tumor had been found on the right side of my colon. (Thankfully, I was still on drugs when my doctor told me the news.) That afternoon, Dr. Bob Wolhman, wanted me to have surgery, that day, to remove the tumor, but I choose to go home. I had to process the information. The next day, Dr. Wolhman gave me names of two surgeons he recommended. I intuitively chose the one who was a miracle himself: Dr. Martin Herman, the offspring of two holocaust survivors.

That evening, my Father gave me the ancient priestly blessing of the Cohanim and said with complete *emunah* (innate conviction that transcends reason) that I would make it. The energy behind his blessing gave me the courage to face the operation, which took place on January 14, 2009. I walked into pre-op laughing, and with so many people, the nurses told us to leave, they were prepping a patient for surgery.

During the operation, the tumor, three feet of my colon, my appendix, and twenty-six lymph nodes were removed. Afterward, my small intestine was connected to my transverse colon. After thirty-six hours, I stopped my pain meds. The nurses were worried about me refusing the morphine. I had to, as I could not control my clairvoyance and was seeing so many spirits I almost lost my mind.

Narcotic drugs can blow a psychic's web open, involuntarily and temporarily paralyzing their will, so they cannot shut it. We may see things between dimensions; in my case, I saw what else was roaming the hospital rooms. Sometimes, a soul will wander on Earth after its body has perished. There are many reasons for this, beyond the scope of this first book. At any rate, it was tripping me out.

By the morning of the sixth day after my operation, I'd had enough. I was sick of the aura of my room and especially fed up with being fed through an IV. My veins were collapsing from all the needles and I was thirsty. So naturally, I threatened to pull out the IV if the nurses would not give me something to drink. They took me seriously. Once the IV was removed, I relaxed. My new colon made a noise, which earned me some green tea, my first meal. A few days later, I was released to return home. Not long thereafter, I decided to write a book about what I have learned, having experienced the other side.

**Learning to Stay Grounded**

Months after the resection surgery, following a deep meditation in prayer, I felt myself go into a mystical state. Becoming very sleepy, I decided to lie down for a while, and fell asleep in my sunny bedroom, filled with light. Suddenly, I was aware that *I* was a light, dancing out of my body. Once again, I looked down at my body asleep on the bed and felt ecstatic to be free of it. It was beyond any physical experience I had ever felt. Every part of my being was vibrating. I danced until I heard a voice commanding me to return to my body. I, who was the soul, continued to dance with sheer joy. I heard the command a second time. Unable to resist it, I sunk down into my body and fell back asleep, almost against my soul's will. (The voice was too strong for me but, thankfully, Heaven was not ready for me yet.)

Several years later on the Day of Atonement, during a prayer break, I spoke with a veteran in the synagogue. Due to wounds sustained in the war, he had survived two near-death encounters. For several years afterward he had vivid dreams that his soul would leave his body and enter the upper world. The experiences did not upset him. He would be told it was not his time yet, and then he would fall back into his body, sometimes with a thud.

One day, as I experienced, his encounters stopped altogether. Both of us surmised it was due to the greater connection we made with our community. For me, walking in the woods was only a part of keeping grounded. I began to volunteer for the children's program in my synagogue, as a storyteller and by taking the children outside to play. I once had twenty-two children ranging in ages from two to twelve. I must admit I was not above bribing them with ice popsicles and joked I was the child tamer. For that hour and a half, as anyone knows who has been around children, there was no spiritual flying; I was in the moment, period. It was a life-affirming gift and I took this opportunity to stay in the present. After that day, my out-of-body experiences abruptly stopped.

I share this story with you to remind you to look at your fingerprint right now. No one else has the same one. It is your special purpose to fulfill here on earth. Do not seek or wish to go into the light until it is your time. You still have work to do; otherwise you would not be here, reading this. And for all we know, as I write this in what is your past, it is to remind you to be in the present. No matter how hard it seems right now, stay here and live. There is always hope—look at me.

## The Search for Meaning

*"Everything is by Divine Providence. If a leaf is turned over by a breeze, it is only because this has been specifically ordained by G-d to serve a particular function within the purpose of creation."*
Baal Shem Tov

We often use dreams to help us make sense of our lives. Who has not searched for a reason as to why things happen? More often than not, things do not make sense—especially when they break our hearts. But sometimes a veil parts and we are given a glimpse of truth. What would change in your life, if you had proof that your soul is eternal? That you live again? Would you still live your life as you do now?

Every soul makes a contract before she enters this world: to be holy. Our mission is to fulfill it. When someone comes to me battling a situation that drains him or her spiritually and emotionally, I ask, "Is this why you were created? Is this your Divine purpose? To waste your moments with negativity and chaos?" Of course the answer is *no*, so I advise them this: Every day, seek out the Creator. Plead your case. Ask that you be guided in the Master Architect's ways, to accomplish what you came here to do. Do this diligently and consistently and you will begin to feel differently, and your life will take on new meaning.

In 2009, the night before life-saving surgery, my friend—an energetic healer—flew up to Seattle to help me prepare. While she worked on my energy, I had a vision that I was walking on a hill in Jerusalem. I knew intrinsically that it was around two thousand years ago. This was not the first time I had seen this image. I had dreamt it in some manner, frequently, since I was in my teens. But this time I was semi-awake and the vision was in vivid detail down to the smell of the cypress trees surrounding me.

Several weeks later, while I recovering at home, the dream went further. In a particular scenario, I found myself captured by Romans and dragged in chains to an area surrounded by stone. My captors believed I had special powers and commanded me to use them to predict the outcomes of their wars. However, I was unable to read their maps or fully understand their language. I woke up from this nightmare sweating and in a panic.

As this dream persisted and deepened, I did not know what to make of it. There was nothing I could do to prevent these nighttime horrors or to alter them. Not even lucid dreaming, a tactic I normally used to control my dreams, worked. I thought this was perhaps a result of PTSD from my recent ordeals. After three months of the dreams steadily growing and playing out, I finally saw the end of the dream:

There were two hundred of us, lined up in a temple. I could see the backs of the Romans in front of us. Somehow I knew that in the future they would reincarnate wearing a symbol I recognized as a swastika. We were threatened, and some of us were beaten. They shouted that two of us would be spared. I was taken to a deranged king; I threw myself at his feet and pleaded for my people. I told him I had special ability and would use it if he would spare my family. Suddenly, I was thrown outside into the night. Jerusalem was on fire and people were running in all directions. The stripes of their robes were smeared with ash and blood. Once again I was captured by the Romans and dragged and paraded in the streets of a place I did not recognize. At this point, I realize that it was year five. I woke up.

Perplexed by the elusive meaning of this latest nightmare, I sought the council of Rabbi Berry Farkash, a Hasidic Rabbi, to help me with the interpretation. He did some research on my lineage and emailed me the following day with his results:

> *The Kahn (Kahana) family, from the Sighetu Marmaţiei region of western Romania, come from a very special priestly family (Cohanim)— one of the ancient families descending from King David and can be traced back all the way to the tribe of Judah. Tradition says that they descended from one of the four noble families of Judah and Jerusalem, the Tapuchim ("Apples" in English). In year seventy, with the destruction of the Second Holy Temple in Jerusalem by the Romans, led by King Titus Tatius, the Kahana family were taken as war spoils, along with many other priestly families. By year seventy-one, they were force to march through the streets of Rome in chains as part of King Titus's victory parade.*

My dream started to make sense; these truly were memories from a past life, windows into the spiral of time. Everything matched up in a way that I never could have made up or imagined—everything but the year. Now I am all about accuracy, so this one small inconsistency—the difference of dates—always bothered me.

Many years later, I watched a documentary on Masada, an ancient fortress on the edge of the Judean desert, which finally brought an answer to the discrepancy of dates. In Masada, archaeologists uncovered a large reserve of coins bearing Hebrew inscriptions reading "Jerusalem the Holy", "Shekel of Israel", "The Freedom of Zion", and "The Redemption of Zion", along with the year of minting, dating from year one to year five. These 'Masada coins' date back to the revolution in Jerusalem from 66CE to 70CE. Led by Judah the Prince, Jewish Zealots rose against the Roman occupation and destruction of Jerusalem. The coins were made every year of the revolt as a symbol of courage and hope that the Romans would be overthrown. This was not to be so, as in the year 70 CE, the Romans destroyed the Second Holy Temple. The Great Revolt ended, and the Jews were killed, exiled, or enslaved. A small minority were captured and taken in chains to Rome.

Finally, a revelation!!!! I now had full verification of my reincarnation. Furthermore, I now understood the nature of my nightmares. These were visions of events that took place in year 70CE, year 5 of the Great Revolt, as the Jews were rounded up and brought to Rome. I was one of those individuals.

## The Spiral of Time

I was allowed to remember that ancient lifetime in order to heal and repair in this one. G-d created a variety of human beings, each which their own gifts to share with the world. I was born once more into the priestly lineage of the Cohanim in order to experience and abide by the commandments of my lineage. These practices hold the key to my purpose and fulfillment in this world. In turn, I offer what I have learned in order to help others uncover the light in their own challenges and find their purpose:

- We reincarnate into the families that can best serve our mission in life. Embrace the ancestry you are born into, unless you are truly called otherwise.
- The Master of the Universe speaks *all* languages. We are *all* his children.
- Each of us is tested with both a good and evil inclination. Not even a saint is without this duality. G-d gives us free will to decide which to follow. We are tested in order to throw us off our real mission here, which is to repair ourselves.
- We must take inventory and remove self-defeating patterns from our thoughts, speech, and action. For example, dissatisfaction, anger, depression, laziness, and fear derive from the evil inclination, keeping us stuck so we lose sight of the big picture.

The following exercise should greatly help you break free of negative thoughts and habits, thereby facilitating connection with your life's *tikkun* (correction). This will also activate your inner strength to keep going when you feel defeated.

## Dreams and Reincarnation

Should you have a reoccurring dream for years in which you experience another life in a different time, it is highly probable that you are seeing a part of your past life. In Kabbalah, reincarnation is referred to as *gilgul*, meaning 'wheels' or 'cycles'. In simple terms, the soul comes back multiple times to rectify what it was unable to fulfill in a previous life. Though it might not feel so, this is truly a blessing from above. A *gilgul* gives a chance for the soul to repair and enables her to elevate higher in her consciousness than in a previous lifetime. When you experience these dreams, it means that your soul is communicating to your intuition that which you were unable to complete in your past life.

Usually, children from the ages of three to eight will remember past lives much more frequently than adults. These visions will come in the form of dreams or nightmares. For instance, a child might dream that they are in a war, or sailing the high seas. How do you know if these dreams are the result of too much television or something from present media or if they are remembering something? What do you do about it?

- Do not judge!
- It is best not to bring up reincarnation with them or in any way to relay to them the possible nature of their visions. Instead, listen attentively and be patient and positive. Tell them it is just a dream, but take not for the future.
- If they come to you with the idea that they lived before, listen and say 'how interesting!' Do not verify nor deny. Just observe and be supportive of your child. Most likely, as your child ages, these dreams will pass. Do not encourage it; they are too young to comprehend.

Adults tend not to experience dreams of past lives. This could be for many reasons; life is tough enough, who needs to revisit the past! However, if something keeps coming back to you, there is a message. When adults do experience dreams of a past gilgul, they can recall the scenario vividly. Sometimes, the dreams in an adult's life are reoccurring in times of extreme emotions or traumatic events. It is important to know that everyone who is in your life is there for a reason: to release or repair. Whatever you are seeing from a past life is something you are supposed to grow and move on from. Children are less judgmental of their dreams than adults and will not dwell on them like an adult will. Especially when there is no underlying issue in the present and when their home life is stable.

- Be positive; you have come back here to complete what you could not before, no matter how tragic it was. You have been given another chance! Heaven wants you to be whole.

**Thoughts to Consider**

- Every interaction we have is part of an infinite puzzle to help repair and elevate the world. Therefore, no one can see the larger picture. Do not assume that people that are difficult in your lifetime are here to punish you for past misdeeds or wrongs.
- It is good to speak to a trusted advisor who will not judge you.
- Do not let your waking moments be consumed with thoughts of your dreams!

- Do not use your knowledge as a crutch, for attention, or to avoid living life in the present moment.
- Continue living your life in the present. If you dwell on this too much, it's like freezing one frame of a movie and thinking it will teach you the whole plot.
- You have been given a gift of awareness; do be compassionate on yourself and others. Remember, we are not the Ultimate Power. If G-d gives us free choice, then surely, we can do the same. Most of us subconsciously feel incomplete and can blame ourselves for the choices of others. The alternative is an unending uphill battle and will not help repair past or present trauma.
- Know that even the worst visions are there to inspire you. This is another chance to have a different outcome, within yourself and what you can control, not what you cannot.

I myself have had many such dreams of past life. Initially, they upset me to no end. Once my Rabbi could pinpoint the reason for my dreams, I clearly heard the message about my path in this life: to celebrate my faith and its commandments. Later speaking with Nechama about the specific details of my dreams of past lives, she helped me peacefully resolve a lifelong pattern. Now, I have a better understanding of my clairvoyant abilities: I have been given them so that I may help guide others.

Be slow to judge your dreams, and do not overanalyze! Let's say you have dreams where you are a great queen or pilot or farmer, and in the current lifetime you work at a grocery store. This is not to say that what you are doing now is not what you are meant to do. It only implies that you were unable to fulfill a piece of your purpose in that lifetime. Perhaps the person standing in your checkout line is someone you were meant to inspire or be kind to in a past life, and you might never even realize it. The people in our lives are here for a reason, and while we cannot control their behaviors, we can control our own. Be mindful of those people to whom you have strong initial reactions. More than likely, you were here with them before. That does not necessarily mean you are meant to be best friends or partners. Maybe you should move on. It might be that simple.

### Liberation

Reincarnation teaches us that, while our soul is immortal, our body is not. The heart beats a finite amount of times and then it stops. Mystics and saints contemplate this truth by aspiring to connect with the Divine in all that they do, so when the moment does come, they can transition with courage and peace. When you find yourself in a situation that makes you feel dissatisfied or depressed, think about the beat of your heart. When you find yourself engaged with those who are hurtful or abusive, let the beat of your heart remind you to love and be kind. We only have only so many heartbeats; why waste them on negativity?

Whatever your past life was or was not; the good news is you are here now! Make a clean start, a fresh slate. Use it wisely. It is your life, no one else's. This is not selfishness but empowerment to action. Be aware of the gifts that come back with you. Take my word for it. It is not worth waiting for something dramatic or traumatic to give you a refresher course. Break free of negative thoughts and habits, to connect with the Divine plan and activate inner strength to keep going when you are afraid. Your dreams will help you understand where you are in your quest.

## Tyger Teachings to Elevate Mood and Thought
*"If you believe that you can damage, then believe that you can fix."*
Rabbi Nachman of Breslov

After years of working with thousands of people, I have come to believe that depression is not limited to just a physical imbalance, but also a spiritual sickness. The solution, while simple, takes courage and discipline. Yet, we can survive even the darkest place when we know we have a higher purpose that lends meaning to our suffering. Here are some things to elevate one's mood and thoughts:

### Air
When cleansing, some things are so basic that they really are just common sense, such as opening a window to let fresh air circulate. Do this daily, even (at least briefly) in winter, to quickly purify your space. It is absurd that at this point in our social development, fresh air and natural light are still not priorities in hospitals or offices. We can become agitated from picking up the energy of others, and this can lead to most of the stress in these environments. Opening windows to let in some fresh air, or playing sacred or classical music, can greatly uplift the environment.

I connect strongly with the energy of Sephardic music, some of my favorite being, Yossi Azulay, with his album *Tefilot Prayers II*, and the *Idan Raichel Project*. Along with a recording, a friend gave me of a Moroccan Kabbalist singing Psalms. I play this at least once a day to cleanse and elevate my surroundings and keep my spirit uplifted. The classics like Mozart, Chopin, Debussy, and (my all-time favorite) "Aquarium" by the French Romantic composer Camille Saint-Saëns *(The Carnival of the Animals)*. The colors that emit from the sounds of notes are out of this world.

**Tyger Tip: Classical Radio**
Music is vibratory and impacts its environment. Even those who are deaf can feel music. Playing classical music will create positive energy, which benefits all inhabitants, including plants and animals. Even the walls absorb sound, so whether you are present or not, keep the radio on. The classical music will bring a feeling of warmth and calmness to any area it is played and will help create a positive atmosphere.

**Water**
Water can be an active force in healing our bodies and souls. Immersing in water helps us become more intuitive through purification and the tranquility that follows this ritual. During the Flood, the only animals that survived were those that dwelled in water. Fresh, moving water purifies energetically because it is derived from the water of Heaven.

The *mikveh*, Hebrew for "collection of water," is an ancient purification ritual that consists of immersing oneself completely, in either fresh, moving water, or within a bath of 1,000 liters that has an opening to let rainwater in. This is done to nullify the ego before the

Eternal One, and calm that animal soul! The immersion ritual calls for an individual to be completely clean of any *chatzitza*, or barrier, to your natural form. These include dirt, jewelry, and clothes. In traditional Judaism, women immerse once a month after the menstrual cycle and men every Friday before the Sabbath. The sages tell us the benefits of the *mikveh*, are multiple: purifying of mind, body, and spirit. Certainly, who has not felt better after a dip in the ocean or clean lake?

Try this exercise if you can: dip yourself from head to toe, ten times in moving water such an ocean or lake. This cleanses the negativity that has accumulated from speech, thoughts, actions, or environment. When on a paddleboard or boat, you are free from the energetic imprint of the landmass. Sailing or floating on water can kindle relaxation, in part, because water demonstrates the natural rhythms of life. This ebb and flow teaches the benefit of adaptability, which can translate to the ups and downs of life. If one is mindful, one can produce a similar effect on a dock. Only semi-attached to land, it is a great place to meditate or collect one's thoughts and breathe.

A rain bath is a similarly wonderful way to cleanse one's mind and spirit, especially when the head is uncovered. Living in the northwest is perfect for this! Additionally, I say my prayers as I am walking in the rain. It is one of the best things to do to invigorate the mind and soul!

The Sages tell us that when there is drought in the land, it is because we are not being kind to each other. Water is aligned with the energy of mercy. Indeed, natural disasters can be attributed to harmful actions to one another that have accumulated to a breaking point—and not necessarily in the places where the actions took place. For instance, rage in the south can cause a destructive situation in the west. In the same manner, an act of mercy in the east can neutralize potential natural disasters from occurring in the north. Every individual's deeds and actions, no matter how small, are key to our planet's welfare. It can restore balance and equanimity or sow destruction.

It is our choice.

Never underestimate the power of your actions. Consider carefully if you really need to "let someone have it," or defend your right to express your anger. Kabbalah tells us that Adam, the first man, was created from all four corners of the earth, so that not a single piece of land could claim sole privilege. Ultimately, we all derive from the same Divine source. (More on this in: Setting Intention in Soulful Spaces.)

**Earth**

Like the ocean, the forest purifies us (however, unlike water, with the right tools we can live in the forest indefinitely). Humanity shares something with the earth; spiritually, they are both the lowest level, and yet they are also the most important. Why? Consider this: many traditions speak of Heaven being the ultimate destination. However, this is a limited viewpoint. We have been given life, this moment equipped with a mind and spirit, to help find with solutions to our problems. Not to abdicate, but to take responsibility on why we are here in the first place! Surely, not just to post a selfie on Instagram! We are here to develop a greater relationship with our soul, which will elevate our actions and make the world a better place. So though earth might be the lowest level spiritually, it has the potential to become the highest. Here are some ways to stay grounded and refreshed:

- Sit in an open field with nothing manmade above your head. Your entire aura will relax, and you will feel calmer. Stay at least ten minutes and you will feel as if you have gone on holiday. Why? In busy cities or social settings, we can frequently draw our aura in close for protective purposes. Being in an open field with the sky as your ceiling and nothing else but the elements to rub up against enables our auras to expand.

**Fire**

Why are we drawn to fire? When it is controlled, fire brings warmth and light. It allows people to nourish themselves on many levels. However, when it is out of balance, fire can destroy. Like all elements, that which nourishes can also destroy. In this book, I will not delve into the deeper mystical understanding, as fire is a very advanced topic. Nevertheless, I will offer a few Tyger tips.

- If you are going to light candles, I encourage people to use candles with light hues or soft earth tone.
- You should not relight an old candle when you have gone through the following, as the fire of candles can act like an energetic sponge.
  - Health issues (physical or mental)
  - Times of emotional stress or trauma
  - Times of great sadness

- When you light candles or any fire, do it with the intention of adding illumination to your environment and create a peaceful atmosphere.
- Fire is mystical. Lighting a fire will help a person to connect to something spiritual, so long as their intention is elevated.

**Heavenly Bodies**

Either purchase a telescope, go to an observatory, or stay up late to watch a meteor shower. Looking into the stars helps to elevate your consciousness. Why? It takes you out of your surroundings and helps you refocus on the reality that is beyond our comprehension. Even going to Google Sky to view pictures of our cosmos will help widen our perception.

## Integrated Soul Workout: Enhance Mindfulness
*"You see but you do not observe."*
Sir Arthur Conan Doyle

Everyone and everything in creation can offer us a lesson in life, so long as we are open to recognizing it. But first, we must become mindful. Simple observation in one's own backyard can instill greater awareness. I have personally seen this affect multiple lives in a positive, life-saving manner.

One morning, I decided to walk on path near my residence that I had not frequented, in several months. Located near a nature preserve, my complex houses a large community with over 360 units on site. That day, I was practicing mindfulness, to train my eye, and I walked on the other side of the property. About two minutes into this, I noticed a spectacularly enormous *active* hornets' nest hanging in a bush about fifty feet away! Well aware that G-d directed me *right* there, and also halted my steps in time, I quickly took action and alerted the management. After it was safely taken care of, the report came back. Apparently, these particular hornets were among the most poisonous kind. They bite as well as sting! What a blessing to have seen it and, most importantly, done something about it! It was a good day, and I was grateful!

Later that week, I spotted a beautiful dragonfly of brilliant turquoise with gold gossamer wings that allowed me to come close and take a picture of it! (See the section on Dream Symbols for the dragonfly's symbolic meaning.) You never know what is right in front of you.

### Let Your Soul Take Charge

You take a seat with the intention to meditate for the next twenty minutes. After a few seconds pass, your mind begins to wander. So you reduce the exercise to 10 minutes. Oops, there goes your phone, which you thought was off. It's a text from your mom/boss/ex/client/office, and you are immediately sidetracked. No worries, you are determined. You decide to do five minutes. Okay, three. You feel hungry; well you did sit down, right? You decide to check your texts then nosh. But you remember to be thankful before you put it in your mouth. *Rock star!* In those few seconds of holding back your hungry animal, your soul was in charge! And you maintained awareness of the moment! For just 10 seconds, yes, but it felt good. *I am going to try that again*, you think, and you walk outside.

*Wow, is that rain? That was not on the forecast; thank you G-d! We need this water!* 15 seconds. Hug your loved one (four-legged ones count too!).

Anything can be a prayer when you are mindful. Judaism has prayers for seeing a rainbow, smelling nice fragrances, seeing a great friend after a long absence, even a prayer to give thanks for the ability to relieve waste! Translation below:

> *Blessed are you, Lord our G-d, king of the universe, who has formed humanity in wisdom and created within him (man) numerous orifices and cavities. It is revealed and known before the Throne of Your Glory that if but one of them were to be blocked or one of them were to be opened, it would be impossible to exist (even for a short while). Blessed are You, Lord who heals all flesh and performs wonders.*

CHAPTER EIGHT

# The Sabbath Experience

## The Desert

After many years of training and assisting the ashram as a medical intuitive, it started taking its toll on my health. I began to have a recurring dream: *I walked into a building with four levels. On each floor, there was a ner tamid* (everlasting light) *hanging above a Torah scroll that was open on a bimah* (alter). *I stood in the doorway looking at the light surrounding these things.* I woke up and said, "One day I will leave the meditation school and follow the footsteps of my ancestors." It took years but eventually I did leave the ashram.

When we begin a process of self-realization of our true path in life, we may find ourselves in a spiritual desert, where we feel isolated from that which we engaged with before. The encampment and feelings of loneliness could last weeks, months, or even years. Do not despair. When you thirst in the desert, your internal longings make you cry out for transformation—that is how change happens in your life. Everything has a shelf life, including suffering.

For instance, the Israelites had to wander through the desert for forty years instead of a few days. Why? They had been an enslaved nation for centuries; it would take a generation to rid themselves from their slave mentality to *learn* to become free.

In their travels, the Israelites set up camp forty nine times. This meant constructing and deconstructing a temporary dwelling of almost a million people. All the while, they were battling internal and external forces, including civil unrest and the encroachment of other nations. Yet, with all the balagan (chaos), they managed to prosper under the direction of Moses, the nation's spiritual leader and prophet. Through his merit and connection to the Divine, many miracles occurred. His sister, Miriam, a great prophetess in her own right, had a miraculous well, a rolling rock that providing fresh water to drink. This well irrigated not only the people and livestock, but the land as well. They created oases for further generations, as well as transforming themselves.

We can still apply this story to modern day. There are periods where things are good. All is well; we are happy, enjoying ourselves, going along for the ride. Then an event occurs and shatters our dreams, whether individually or collectively: war and betrayal, terrorism, disease, environmental issues, natural disasters, etc. Reeling from the shock, we scramble to move forward, but are unable. What can we do?

- Decide, no matter what you are experiencing, that you will find meaning in it. Even if it is simply to prevent others from making the same mistake.
- Stay strong! Know that this encampment is temporary.
- Find a way to be like Miriam and her well of water. Irrigate the desert:
    o Give the water you are seeking.
    o If you are unemployed: While job-hunting for yourself, also be open to help others network. Your kindness will move energy and break the stagnation.

- o If you are searching for your soul mate: Be on the lookout to help someone else find his or her match.
- o If you are medically challenged: Give to charity and consistently pray for the full recovery of someone in need.
- o If you are praying for children: Pray that others should be blessed with a child; volunteer and spend time with children.

We can learn so much as we go through our own encampments. Do not assume that your travails and hardships are for naught. You are becoming purified through them and what it means to be free. We might never know how many lives we touch in the process. Certainly it is never one's choice to suffer, but it can take some practice to learn otherwise. Whatever the situation, you choose how you react to it! As Viktor Frankl—neurologist, psychiatrist, and holocaust survivor from Austria—writes in his book, *Man's Search for Meaning*, "Everything can be taken from a man but one thing: the last of the human freedoms—to choose one's attitude in any given set of circumstances, to choose one's own way."

## Sabbath: Oasis in the Desert

The ancient ritual of *the Sabbath*—taken from the Hebrew word, *Shabbat*, meaning to 'sit' or 'rest'—is a practical way to address the needs of our bodies while feeding the soul. More than that, it nourishes every level of your being. Taking a weekly sabbatical to rest benefits your mind, emotions, and body, and nourishes the soul. The Sabbath benefits all of humanity, regardless of whether you are Jewish or not.

The lesson of the Sabbath is moderation, discipline, training ourselves to experience joy, and elevating the mundane in every aspect of humanity. It is a blueprint for having a spiritual experience in the body. This blueprint is not only for humanity, but for the earth as well. From an environmental point of view, on the Sabbath, a person refrains from driving and using electronics. What a great way of conserving energy and reducing our carbon footprint! According to the Torah, we are commanded to rest the land every seventh year (a practice called *shemittah*—the original Earth Day!) so the soil is not depleted.

The Sabbath traditionally begins Friday at sundown and ends at nightfall the next day. For others, it begins and ends on Sunday. On it, we cease all creative work and spend time enriching our souls. From the book of Genesis, we learn that the Master of the World completed creation in six days and took the seventh day as a day of rest. As Divine beings, why would we do anything less than our Creator? Humanity needs consistent, weekly time-outs to reconnect with what is essential in life, regardless of what nation you are a part.

Kabbalah states that on the Sabbath, the *Shekinah* (the feminine aspect of G-d) is brought down. Tradition calls for men and women to prepare their homes to welcome the Shekinah with respect and joy, as one would prepare for a queen or bride. Kabbalists wear white and are encouraged to use this color on the table to signify the sanctity of the island of time one is about to enter.

Before the onset of the Sabbath, women traditionally light candles to bring in the Light of the *Shekinah.* Through their lighting, the household knows that the Sabbath has begun. This window of time is an opening for prayers to be answered. Single or married, old or young, all women have the ability to call in the Light and set the spiritual tone for their homes.

One does not have to be Jewish to call for the light. We are all creations of G-d.

## Sabbath: Encampment of Peace

The following are the basic Kabbalistic rituals of Shabbat that have been practiced, unbroken for thousands of years.

There is a special song called *Shalom Aleichem* (Hebrew for 'peace be upon you all') that is conventionally sung three times before the Sabbath meal on Friday night. In it, you invoke four angels of the Eternal One to come to your table, bless everyone, and to go out to the world in peace before the meal starts. This is to allow blessing to come into your home, while at the same time keeping the intimate atmosphere for you to reconnect with the Omnipresent and recuperate from your stressful week.

After the singing, it is time to begin the meal, which begins with *Kiddush* over wine. Traditionally, men will make the blessing, but women can take over if necessary. As the word, *kiddush*, means 'holy' or 'separate', this *mitzvah* (commandment) allows the special sanctity of the Sabbath to come into the home.

Everyone is encouraged to wash their hands with a ritual cup and blessing to further sanctify him or herself. Then, *challah*, braided bread that is baked specifically for Shabbat, is blessed and shared. A wonderful meal begins, with positive, uplifting conversation. Because of the inherent joyful attitude that comes with Shabbat, singing and dancing might break out. (This happens in mine. The mitzvah is not only to rest, but also be joyous, which I try to fulfill— and I love to dance!) When the meal is finished and the after blessing has been said, the resting portion of Sabbath begins.

The next day, we continue feeding our soul by refraining from work, errands, and any mundane activity. We focus on rest and spiritual integration by spending time in the present with our family or friends and playing games, learning, or taking a walk. Some will nap most of the day; after all we are commanded to rest! (Can you believe it is considered a mitzvah to take a nap on a Saturday afternoon? If only everything else was this simple! Many relationships have been transformed because of this custom.)

When three stars appear in the sky, it signifies that Shabbat is over and a new week has begun. We enter with light, and we exit with light, in a ceremony called *Havdallah*. Here, we take the energy of the Sabbath to illuminate the rest of the week. The goal is to emerge refreshed and inspired.

**How to Begin Keeping Shabbat**

I recommend starting slowly. Decide to make Friday night dinner. Make it distinctive. Buy flowers, cook a special dinner ahead of time, and use your best dishes. Use a tablecloth (I prefer white) to serve as a reminder to separate the energy of the week and to elevate your table. Put your phone and other electronics away in another room. Most importantly, invite company to share this meal with; even one person will help create the atmosphere.

Before Shabbat commences, light your candles, and take a moment to recognize the beauty that you have brought and welcomed into your home.

Eventually, work your way towards keeping the full twenty-five hour period. Every moment of keeping Shabbat is a blessing. If you can only keep one hour, this is still an amazing accomplishment. Each experience builds from the previous. Shabbat is like a breath of fresh air and a delight for the soul. When a person commits to keeping the Sabbath, the gifts that come from this are a sense of feeling grounded, connected, and rejuvenated. It is a weekly time out to get reacquainted with your loved ones, as well as your soul.

CHAPTER NINE

# Prayer and the Forest

*"Keep in mind the essence of your prayers is the faith you have in them, that they will be answered . . ."*
Rabbi Nachman of Breslov

Higher and lower worlds exist in parallel to us—not above or below—in dimensions that vibrate faster or slower. Kabbalah tells us that in order to access the plane where miracles exist, all we have to do is "go one cubic higher" with our thoughts and actions. Of course, this is easier said than done, especially for those who feel they are swimming in quicksand. Still, it is imperative everyone finds a way. A key component of the journey is prayer.

Four months after the operation to remove the tumor in my colon, my fingernails started to break off. My doctors thought it was my body's way of reacting to what I had been through. But my twin, Tovah, who was in Chicago thousands of miles away, felt something was wrong. New tests revealed I needed an iron transfusion immediately. Once again it was a Friday, a full moon, and the hospital was jumping, just like the night my sister and I were born and the Friday night I was reborn when I received my life-saving blood transfusion.

Though I had a bed, it was a nerve-wracking eight hours before they even began the procedure. Because I was so thin, two nurses placed heat packs on my arms to keep the veins open and the IV from failing. I started to despair. I could hear a woman screaming in the room next door, suffering from the effects of brain cancer. The nurses were concerned her agony was freaking out the other patients but no drug could calm her. My intuition told me her soul, not her body, was causing the distress, and when no one was looking, I had Joseph wheel me in to speak with her. She was sitting up, screaming, while male nurse tried to coax her into lying down. For a few moments our eyes met. Through this connection, I told her that she was not alone. As I reached out to her, a nurse came and brought me back to my room. But the floor became quiet and so did the woman, who gave me the courage to lie there for the next six hours while my body absorbed the iron.

Yet there was beauty. *I saw more angels in pediatrics ICU, around the children, than I had ever seen anywhere else.* It was heaven and hell occupying the same space. But no matter what, G-d is always there.

Even in the darkest situation we find ourselves, remember this:

> *There once was a young orphan who set off on a journey to meet the Greatest King That Ever Existed. The King lived in a tremendous castle on the Highest Mountain, beyond an ocean of fiery blue waters, slippery and breakable as glass. So determined was the orphan's desire to meet the King, the boy managed to move across the waters without burning. When he reached a valley of flowers, it was so intoxicating and fragrant that, for a moment, he forgot his own name (never mind the reason for the journey). Suddenly, a*

*thorn amidst the flowers pricked his finger and drew blood, breaking the spell of his amnesia.*

*He trudged onwards through cold moons and icy deserts, until he reached a road surrounded by trees with leaves of smoking white fire. Finally, the castle was in view! But the front door was forty-nine gates away! This was too much even for a willful boy; he started to cry heavy sobs. Suddenly, a single wooden bench appeared and the boy sat down to rest. From the corner of his eye, he spied a book sitting next to him wrapped in velvet. As he reached over and opened it, words fell out; words wrapped in tears and laughter. They were the names of the parents he never knew, as well as all the creatures and wondrous sights from his journey and, most importantly, his own name in gold! His laughter, tears, and exclamations of joy had all been recorded in the book! They spilled from the pages, and danced before his eyes. That's when he realized he had already met the King. In every creature and sound of creation, the King and his Queen were there with him.*

## Praying and Healing in Nature

*"When a person meditates in the fields, all the grasses join in his prayer and increase its effectiveness and power."*
Rabbi Nachman of Breslov

Going into nature aligns our body with our soul, as it immerses us in the handiwork of our Creator.

Certain healing energies, physical and spiritual, can be found in specific places where nature thrives. Ideally, we should learn to create this atmosphere within all geographical areas: rain forests, woods, and mountains, even deserts. There are millions of healing plants around the world, with new ones being discovered every day. Hopefully we will one day learn to respect the Divine pharmacy and support her, taking measures to ensure the continuation of our planet.

As we live in a noisy world, spending time in nature can help to give relief to our nervous systems. Many times I have turned to immersing in nature to inspire my mind, soul, and body. For example, when I was recovering from surgery in Washington, I discovered a special place near my home called (seriously) Tiger Mountain. While I walked amidst the evergreens, I poured my heart out in gratitude for my life.

Our physical body requires what is derived from nature in order to survive. Our spiritual body needs to connect with a higher power in order to thrive. No one can do this for you; it must come from within, through greater soul awareness, which happens in nature.

**Sound**
When you go to a place where nature thrives, instead of hearing the typical daily assault of beeps, buzzing, humming, and loud talking, you are exposed to a more natural type of sound. These noises are more integral to your makeup, as they reflect the inherent world of our plant. Being surrounded in nature therefore helps your nervous and sensory systems to relax and be rebooted. In turn, this will help activate your intuition.

Specific areas around the head can work like radio antennas, picking up sensory signals that can be deciphered and translated into meaningful information. Most people are unaware of this. Don't believe me? Try this experiment: next time you feel overloaded by external stimulus, cover your head. It will muffle the receptors on these radio chakras, helping to tone things down and allow you to become centered. Covering the head also helps with elevating our thoughts from the mundane by remind us there is a greater world above our heads—and ego's desires.

Sound either diminishes or expands intuition, depending on the composer and instrument. Sound can take us to higher places spiritually as well as mentally. Take Mozart's music for example: Mozart's savant abilities are well documented; he certainly was accessing a very special part of the brain that is asleep for most of us. Frequent exposure awakens and activates parts of our brains used for cognitive functions as well as intuitive thought. Studies have indicated that consistent listening to Mozart opens up neural pathways in the brains. This is also true of other classical composers. These works train our ear to recognize compositions of sounds, composed by a highly creative being. This exposure can also assist with developing intuitive skills, as it helps us to become aware of harmonious patterns, perfect timing, and interconnectedness.

The night of my near-death experience, I heard the words '*Ribbono Shel Olam*' over and over, which translates to 'Master of the Universe'. The words were so palpable; I had no doubt that it was truth. Much later, I found out that it was the most frequently used prayer of

Rabbi Nachman of Breslov. Intuitively, I practiced his prayer method of *hitbodedut* (self-seclusion), where a person is encouraged to go out to the fields and speak to our Divine Parent in their own language. Nothing is meaningless or trivial! It is okay to pour your heart about your date, your pet, or even the person who cut in front of you. It might even make you laugh when you do!

**Anatomy of a Prayer**

*"Oh Lord, my G-d, I pray that these things never end,*
*The sand and the sea,*
*The rush of the waters,*
*The crash of the Heavens,*
*The prayer of Man."*
*Hannah Szenes*, 1921–44, a courageous heroine

The Jewish people have prayed for thousands of years in a three-part manner: The first is praise to the Supreme Being, the second is the request—healing, health, knowledge, money, and the final part is thanksgiving. As Rabbi Berry Farkash told me, "In Judaism, we believe that the second you request from the Ultimate Source in prayer, you could already give thanks because you already have it. You have already changed the whole setting in your life. Do not underestimate this regular, ordinary, systematic— maybe not even inspirational—type of prayer; it can completely shift our reality."

Prayer transmutes your past, alters your present, and shifts your future. It is transformative and redemptive, giving us the ability to change our moment.

It surpasses predictions. You can change your future when you connect with the Divine.

## Nature's Language

Everything in creation has a language through which it can make requests to the Maker. For instance, frogs have been given a song that sings for rain. While most beings are unable to decipher this, there is the rare occasion when someone can. Interestingly enough, it is said that some of my ancestors, including King Solomon and the Baal Shem Tov (blessed be their names), could hear these languages. It is even said that they could understand the language of the trees as well. Certainly, I am not even a smidgen close to this level. However, through careful observation of the language of the forest, I have gained the following insights:

- If you see white butterflies tinged with yellow, there will light rain; with blue, it will be heavy. When they fly within a close personal radius it is a good sign; your soul is emanating positive vibrations. Should they land on you, it is a sign that you are in a merciful state. Why? If you observe a butterfly, they are in constant motion. When they do rest, it is on flowers or foliage, things known for their beauty and nourishment. So, when a creature like a butterfly rests on you, it means you embody these qualities (in the moment).

- If you hear crickets during the day in a succession of two, then expect temperature to rise and humidity to drop. Crickets normally come out at night. When you hear them loudly in the day, expect humidity to drop and temperatures to rise significantly. While I was living in California, it was my go-to method for determining when the Santa Ana waves were coming.

- When deep red mushrooms grow in early fall, it will be a cold but dry winter. If the mushrooms are white or beige, it will be less frigid and significantly wet.
- When it rains in the north, it is clear in the south, and vice versa.
- When temperatures rise in the East coast, they drop in the West Coast, and vice versa.
- The oceans and lakes serve as a mirror for collective consciousness. When they are not healthy, neither are we.

The natural world will always give you a weather report more accurate than that of the weatherman, no matter the new technology and climate devices. If a person were to spend some time observing the natural world, they would know what the seasons were going to bring and could prepare accordingly.

**Renewal of Winter**
Both animals and trees seem to know when a cold winter is developing, growing thick coats of fur or moss around their trunks or branches in the fall. I have seen this enough times over several years to know that it is more than a coincidence. A heavy snowfall can purify the forest and landscape. Remember what I said about rainfall? Snow is simply frozen water. In the cold winter, the forest is celebrating! (To my eyes at least.) This simple pleasure can act as a remedy for reclusive, lonely, or fearful people to remove themselves from their heads and house. (Preferably in pairs or more.)

Whether you can perceive energy or not, the spirit is refreshed in nature. If you are physically up to it, walk in the forest in winter; it can be expansive, healing, and exhilarating; well worth bracing for the frigid temperature. I highly recommend it.

**The Language of Trees**

*I dreamt all the plants of the world were holding a council, represented by a beautiful queen. The plants demanded to be withdrawn from the world of man, in response to the destruction inflicted on them by these beings. In defense, the Queen of Compassion advocated for mankind. After heavy debate it was decided that the plants would remain on Earth. Two representatives from the humans were chosen: man's defender and myself, we who understand the language of plants.*

Mystics have long known that when you walk through woods and sense divinity, you are sensing the trees speaking to G-d. Plants occupy our world as witnesses, guardians, and teachers. They provide lessons fundamental to the recipe of the intuitive being: lessons of strength, generosity, truth, and flexibility.

If you listen, you can hear the trees whisper. I have.

It was fall, brisk, and late in the day, yet I just had to be in the woods. By the time I arrived, the wind was kicking up and made the leaves crackle. It was joyous! I knew I did not have much time until it would be too dark to see, so I hurried down the path, exhilarated from the freedom of letting my aura out. (Something like taking off one's shoes and running through the grass.) While walking, I sensed the trees were murmuring about a longed-for second child. Suddenly, their message clicked in my head; I rushed home to call my friend and relay the forest's message. She went silent for a few moments, then began to laugh and said, "I have not even told my husband yet!" It was true! (Later I heard hubby was slightly miffed that the trees knew before he did.) The trees derive from the source in which all source comes from.

There are no secrets . . .

Everything in creation is interconnected. Regardless of where we are in our lives, creation is a witness to our comings and goings. After all, to earth we return, so of course it will recognize us when we return. As Einstein famously observed, energy is never lost, just transformed.

People that take psychedelics and go into nature are doing themselves a disservice. While one might see energetic visions that ordinary sight does not allow. Those who are not spiritualty mature can put themselves in danger. There are certain cultures that have spiritual leaders who will occasionally use herbs and plants to assist them on 'vision quests'. They do so under the tutelage of a spiritual elder. Unless this is your custom, I do not recommend this practice.

When I let my aura "hang out" and soak up the green and blue healing energies of the woods, I pray beforehand, go with a companion, and walk on a path that is used frequently enough for animals to have grown accustomed to humans.

One of my favorites holidays in the Jewish calendar is called Tu B'Shvat, which takes place in winter (late January to early February) as the light returns. On this day, Kabbalah explains that the Souls of the trees awaken from their slumber and the gates of *chessed* and *rachamim* (mercy) open. It is a special time to appreciate and reconnect with nature. Many individuals will plant new trees as a form of renewal and nourishment.

## Exercise: Hear the Whispers of Trees

To learn a new language, it is not enough to study a few times a year. You must be willing to immerse yourself in it, to be patient. It can take years to become fluent. This holds even truer with the language of trees, which come as impressions, more than anything else. For instance, have you ever walked in nature and had a sudden thought come to you, unrelated to what you were thinking? Lifting your mood suddenly lifting to the point that you almost felt high (especially when it is sunny or after a cleansing rain)? You are sensing the gratitude of nature influencing your psyche. The wind carries information and signals that trees receive and store. Gifted and psychic people can place their hands on a tree trunk and pick up impressions of what occurred in the area. Though a rare ability, it is a fun skill to practice. One thing is for sure: you will sense something, if even just great *whoosh* of energy. Of course, be sensible and do not pick a tree that looks diseased or covered in spiders and ants. Select a tree that appeals to you and gently place your hands on it, closing your eyes. Relax there for a few moments, then open your eyes and continue on your walk. Big revelations will not come instantly but over time you will become more sensitive to the tree's language, and your eyes will be opened to the beauty of this world. This simple exercise can provide enhanced appreciation for the work of the Creator and activate inner happiness. Some trees are very old; they were here long before we arrived and will be here when we leave. Eventually our bodies will become part of one.

As you nurture your intuition, I recommend walking the same woods for at least a year. Do not worry about growing bored. The forest is dynamic; it is never the same as the day before. Think about it: if you wanted to learn Portuguese, would you run around from country to country? Or would you find a town, settle down, and listen carefully to the dialect of the villagers for a while? I have walked the same patch of woods for almost seven years, and I *never* grow tired of it. Every leaf, every stone has a story. I have found the more time I spend in one area, the better I become at predicting weather! When I go to a new forest in a different state or country, I have to learn the particular dialect of the landscape all over again. If you do not leave near a forest, then pick a park or any place where nature is growing. It will have the same effect on your mind and spirit.

## Rosh Chodesh: the Rebirth of the Moon

Each month, we have a chance to make a fresh start with our soul's purpose, collectively and individually. This is during the time of the new moon, which in Judaism is referred to as, Rosh Chodesh ("Head of the month" in English). In Kabbalah, the feminine energy is often compared to the moon and its light. During the new moon, the light is hidden from view. Nevertheless, the light still nourishes both our psyches and the planet. This is similar to feminine energy, which its essence is nourishment and growth. Just like Rosh Chodesh is the anchor of the month, so too are women the anchor that guides relationships and the spiritual light in home. Because of the inherent connection to the womb and feminine energy, Rosh Chodesh is often a period of heightened creativity and an excellent time to initiate projects. (There is even an old wives' tale that if you cut your hair on a new moon, it will grow faster than if you cut it at any other time).

The full moon emits light connected with feminine consciousness. As our bodies are largely composed of water, the magnetic pull of the lunar cycle influences not only the tides but humanity as well. We can also feel its effects in our emotional nature, in some cases, beginning as early as three days before and up to two days after. This is why there is often a lot of action in emergency rooms, police stations, and the like around this time.

On a side note, after carefully observing a diverse pool of clients over many years, I have noticed a few important patterns. Opportunities can appear when the phase of the moon is the same as the time of their birth, or if you were born within days of or after a lunar event. For instance, if you were born during a full moon or new moon, blessings may present themselves during this period. Additionally, Kabbalah says that each day of the year has its own energy and connects with the energy of the same day in previous years. On your birthday in the lunar cycle, this energy offers power to your blessings. So be sure to give blessings to all of your friends and family!

**Tyger Teaching: The Day You Entered the World**
There are energies corresponding to each day of the week. They are stronger or weaker, depending on the nature of the day. An individual's birth date will give off a particular energy of productivity. And how naturally so! What was a more auspicious event in your entire life than you birth? You will naturally be more in-tune with the energy of this day, and generally, this can translate as opportunities presenting themselves. It is almost like a cosmic reminder that you are alive for a reason. You will also have a natural affinity and/or challenges with individuals born on the same day as you.

Find out the day you were born. Take a moment and think, on what day of the week do you generally have a little extra pep, or like to make events or do things? You will find, more than likely, that it will correspond to the above. Next time that day of the week arrives, be mindful of this special connection and see how it affects your attitude. For instance, do you know anyone that seems immune to the Monday Blues and seem full of a vigor that's uncharacteristic of everyone else? Bet you they were born on a Monday!

Now find out the dates of your loved ones. Think it through. You will find patterns within your loved ones that can help you understand an aspect of their rhythm. This, in turn, will help you understand your own rhythm and you will become more cognizant of your relationship to them.

**The Intuition Compass**
When I was a child, my family had a cottage where we would spend most of the summer, trading the heat of the city for the cool breeze of the countryside. I always looked forward to these escapades; the summer was the

one time I felt truly free. When I was outside, I could feel a guardian protecting me. I would experience a rush of light run through me; I felt fearless. I would run around outside until dusk, dancing on the grass as the air was cooling and the frogs were singing, the breeze moving through the trees. At night, the fireflies would come out and I would run around the yard attempting to catch them with my bare hands, wanting to capture their light.

The minutes before curfew seemed full of possibilities—if only I could stay outside longer! When darkness would fall I could barely make out the fireflies, I would have to return inside, to wait the next day when I could embark on a new adventure.

**Tyger Tip: True North**

Take a moment; think of when you last felt free, innocent, and safe. This was when your soul and body were at peace. Though you did not realize it, your intuition was available to you. We all have an intrinsic intuitive compass that directs us to true North. Depending on how we live, we can bury or reveal it, like a lost treasure in sand. Why? When we are at peace, the Divine Presence rests with us. At this moment, your higher soul is in charge and is speaking to you. Look at the scenery in this memory, whether it is your childhood home, nature, a favorite location, etc. This will indicate where you feel most comfortable and connected. Do not be afraid if your compass grows or changes, it is meant to. As we evolve and we set new pathways and create new patterns of being, our intuitive compass does the same.

CHAPTER TEN

# Receiving Divine Guidance

Divine guidance can come through dreams, words, books, people—an individual might not even realize it. Be discerning. If you feel a message coming through something, verify the source. Just because something comes your way that seems exciting or like what you thought you wanted does not mean that it is on either count. Great actions attract great forces from both sides of the fence. This is in order to help the soul learn how to choose what is right.

**Passing through the Pit**
In the late nineties, I embarked on a flight bound for L.A. from Palm Beach. As I reached my seat, I knew psychically that one of the engines was malfunctioning. Deciding to take a chance, I went to inform a flight attendant (this was before 9/11). I walked up to first class and, as Divine providence would have it, a pilot emerged from the cockpit. Introducing myself as an astrologer—it sounded better than clairvoyant—I told him the planets were wonky and to check the left engine of the aircraft. (Can you imagine if I did this now? I would probably be arrested.) As the words left of my mouth, an engineer arrived and boarded the plane. The pilot looked at me strangely—it did not help I was wearing a sarong—and told me to return to my seat. Before I did, I let him know we would be switching planes. He laughed and told me to go back and check on the planets, and that we would be taking off shortly.

Thirty minutes later, the pilot announced on the PA that we would be disembarking. One of the aircrafts engines was malfunctioning. In the terminal, I felt someone's eyes on me and an hour later, as I settled into my seat on the new plane, an older man approached me and asked if he could sit down. The plane was pretty empty, but I said, "Sure, why not?" He introduced himself as D and I soon learned he had been a mathematician who had worked for the military, debugging the Internet during its infancy. After that gig, he made a lot of cash as a tech investor. He had been sitting in first class when he overheard my conversation with the pilot and was curious. How had I known something was wrong with the plane?

I told him the truth: I had no idea.

I told him I was a clairvoyant and sometimes just knew things.

We spoke the entire ride back and I shared my dream of doing a documentary on alternative healing. We exchanged emails and kept in touch. Miraculously, a month later, D gave me $75,000 dollars as an investment for my documentary. This was particularly amazing because I had written a check "from the universe" to myself seven months before, which I was carrying around in my wallet!

I was in deep quicksand, only I could not see it . .
.

## The Psychic Surgeon

When I began my documentary, I had no idea what I was doing or how to be a producer. I met many people; most of them charlatans—but fortunately, I could tell this clairvoyantly and did not take them seriously. One fateful day, a friend rang from London and suggested I check out a so-called "psychic surgeon," from the Philippines, to consider for my documentary. It sounded like sheer quackery, but I was also really curious and willful. So, together with two friends—one who published conspiracy theories, and the other who was a young, twenty year old artist—I went to see the 'healer'.

We drove to a gated community in the valley and parked in the driveway of a typical suburban home. Inside, there were about ten people sitting on plastic chairs in a circle around the 'surgeon'. He appeared to be in his late sixties with longish hair. I knew we should leave when I saw his one long dirty fingernail; it was beyond creepy. But, ignoring intuitive red flags going off each second, I waited to meet with him. After he was done reading Bible passages, he left the room. Then guests went, one-by-one, up some stairs for their "healing" session.

When it was my turn, as I walked up the stairs, I heard a voice say loudly and clearly, "Go home!" But I dismissed it and entered a room where the jungle man motioned me onto a bed and told me to close my eyes. I peeked out of one eye and saw a bowl filled with water on the table. The "healer" placed his hands over my abdomen and I felt a strong suction like a high-powered vacuum. Moist warmth ran down my sides; it was freaky, and I refused to look. When he was finished I opened my eyes and saw he was holding the bowl of water. Though he had placed a napkin over it, I could see it was filled with blood. Shocked, I looked down at my body but could not see any openings.

Shaken to my core, I knew something very wrong had taken place. It is not like I had not experienced strange things before. But this was something dark! As I said earlier, most of the people I had interviewed for the documentary were performers, even if they did not realize it. Illusion creates delusion, which is why standards in the esoteric sciences must be maintained at the highest level at all times. We must be careful not to lose a foothold din reality. But this was altogether different. This guy knew exactly what he was doing and it was not good. It really happened: he put his hands through me. I have seen people's futures and received messages from the dead, but this was beyond my comprehension. To this day, I shudder and wish with all my heart I had never gone to see that man. It was a fork in my path that I should never have taken. It took years to recover from the fallout on so many levels that I am grateful to be here. The lesson is, when you hear a voice clearly telling you to go home . . .

Go home.

**Lessons Learned**

- *Healing is a relationship with your body, mind, and soul.* This is a process that requires commitment, courage, and respect. Anyone who promises instant results is delusional or worse. Trust the voice within that doubts the sales pitch.
- *Advocate for your intuition.* If something does not feel right, do not go further. You might never know why you aborted the potential job, relationship, move, etc., but this is better than suffering the consequences later.

- *Your body is truthful.* If it hurts, there is a reason; it is instinctual with a will to live. If answers evade you, fight until they come!
- *The best healers respect their patient's feedback.* Whether traditional or alternative, they will defy conventional treatment with their patients if their intuition tells them to.
  - o Recently, I have had a few doctors in my classes who were interested in further developing this trait. I asked them: If they followed their hunches to conduct further studies on a patient that had tested negative for whatever, did their suspicions prove correct? They all nodded in agreement.
- *Do not compromise your values and integrity for anyone or anything.*

**Respecting Boundaries, or "Let the Dead Rest"**

As my abilities developed, I reached a point where I could hear the dead (which is nothing like what you see on television or in movies). It was not something I sought out; my "antenna" grew excessively amplified by my training and, occasionally, a client would come in for a session and a spirit would simply appear with a message. I was happy to share those messages, and to help in cases where I could identify specific life-saving medical intervention. But passing in and out of worlds is extremely dangerous to the messenger; the medium is always at risk. Certain discarnate beings in the spiritual realms like to pretend to be somebody's relative, for sport or worse. I did my best to avoid this particular type of circumstances. In the few cases that failed, I would put the energy to the test, to ensure authenticity. But let's face it, how can you truly verify—is there documentation? Nevertheless, it was a slippery slope; I was at peril, intuitively, physically, and spiritually.

Around the same time, I used my gifts to help out the police. This was even more intense. By the time a cop goes to consult a psychic, they have run out of options. More than likely, you are going to find a body. I decided to donate my services anyway because I was young and on a mission to save the world. I did not understand the effects that being a "locator" would have on my psyche. Since then, I have learned that it is best to first save yourself, so you have the stability and longevity to truly make an impact.

The last case I worked on for the police was particularly challenging. A woman had gone missing, so her family had hired a private detective who soon ran out of leads. As a last-ditch effort, he came to me for a consultation. No matter how many times I "looked," I had the same vision: I saw a woman with dark hair walking in certain setting. This did not help things because the missing person had red hair. Assuming I had the wrong psychic lead, I worked for days, trying to access additional information. As nothing new developed and time ran out, I passed on the coordinates of the area where I felt the detective should sweep. They eventually found her body in the area I had seen. It was the missing woman in a dark wig, may her soul be blessed. When I heard the news, I cried and cried and thought I had failed to be of service. I was so intent on helping them find a live person. However, I now realize that locating a body nevertheless comforts the soul. That which derives from dust must return to that, from which it came. Respecting the body—even when it is lifeless—is a great act of true service, as it demonstrates unconditional compassion for G-d's creation. Even so, I never again chose to work with a detective.

### The Dangers of Being a Medium

Even over a decade later, speaking to the dead was still a dilemma for me. I could count on one hand the times it occurred and I was *never* comfortable with it, even in a case of a suicide, where I had compassion for the family members who came to me for help. Shortly after my surgery, my monk friend who had moved back to Tibet flew into Seattle for a visit. Since we had been close, I felt I could confide in him. Over lunch I told him about my fears in communicating with the dead and how it affected me. I did not wish to be a medium on any level, though it had been highly encouraged in the meditation school. I wanted to know his thoughts. The monk listened deeply and recommended I continue to speak to the spirits. Not to do so, in his opinion, would be impolite and create negative karma. It was a service to those in need. (Ha! this coming from someone who barely talked to the living on the phone.) I worried that he was right, so I tried timing my encounters, to not be a "receiver" for more than five minutes. That never worked. Let's face it; if a spirit is hanging around and they want to talk, they have all the time in the world. It is not like you can hang up on them or drive away. I had to stop communicating with them entirely if I wanted to remain healthy and sane.

Later, when I spoke with my friend and teacher, Rabbi Berry Farkash, he told me the Kabalistic view on the matter: my decision to stop lined up with my intuition. Life is for the living. If the departed need to communicate, they can visit in a dream or impart a message to your intuition. Which you will get; you can count on that. This might not seem as comforting as seeing a medium, but it is the safest and most authentic way to communicate with a loved one who is no longer in this world. Have you had moments where suddenly you felt better after thinking of them? Even if we are not aware of it, our departed loved ones visit us from time to time. They were most likely sitting next to you, sending vibrations of comfort and love. We can help them as well, especially if they left at a young age. Doing *chessed* in their honor keeps their memory alive and enables them to continue to affect the world in a positive way. There are many levels in Heaven and the dead do not remain stationary. Should we build a school or donate to charity in their name, the act elevates their soul in the upper worlds. It works the other way as well: when miraculous things occur, it is not always due to our karma, but the merit, or *zechut*, we inherited from the deeds of our ancestors.

### A Father's Love

On one occasion, a client with a previous history of cancer came to see me for a reading. She had just been given a clean bill of health by her doctors and came in regarding her career. After I finished invocative prayers, her father, who had died nineteen years previously, appeared to me in a vision and urged his daughter to go back for another check. I shared this with my client and she was not surprised. For weeks previously, she had been having a recurring dream that her father was calling on the phone. She would pick up and either not hear him or not remember what he was saying. After her session with me, she went back to her doctor. This time, they found precancerous cells in her uterus. Thank goodness, they caught it in time! Exactly twenty months later, she gave birth to a son. Her father was clearly impressing a message to his loved one in a dream that she was unable to fully pick up. I do not know if that is why she came to me; however, because it was urgent, her father did not give up. I appreciated the chance to help relay this information. To me, this is different from seeking communication with the dead, which was not my client's goal.

**Channeling**

Another popular subject in esoteric schools, channeling involves allowing a discarnate, a being or beings no longer on this plane of consciousness, to enter one's body and transmit information to the "host." I am not going to debate whether these experiences are "true" or not. However, I will caution that many lost souls wander the earth, posing as all kinds of things with the express desire of finding a body to possess. Because they are no longer of this world, they can access information telepathically. This can seem authentic, but can be completely deceptive. So beware! The ego can trick all kinds of mystical people; some may believe they are channeling a so-called deity. All because they do not know better and think they are helping others.

Guidance comes in many forms. We were made in G-d's image, containing the essence of holiness inside us. Sometimes our teachers are not physical; they may exist in the inner plane of conscious that we can access safely in dreams or, in rare cases, visions. Kabbalah speaks about clear boundaries regarding the vessel we have been blessed with, our bodies. Unless you want to become schizophrenic or possessed, keep your body for yourself. Your body is for your soul alone, not a VRBO (vacation rental by owner) to rent out to spirits.

## Do not Believe Reality TV

Though they probably do not realize it, most (though not all) people who claim to speak to the dead are actually reading your thoughts, particularly the thoughts you have of your loved ones.

If a person of this world is truly speaking to the dead, there are tangible, physical effects, such as interference with technology and changes in temperature. These effects are not subtle and, as this work often is, can be very dangerous to the medium. I have replaced cell phones, laptops, and various other electronics—so much so that it has become a running joke among friends and family. When I was in my twenties, I demagnetized so many of my ATM cards that the bank finally refused to send me more. I had to learn how to dim my clairvoyance, to work more intuitively, and to develop more user-friendly tools, such as working with dreams. Should you have similar experiences, follow this advice:

- Imagine there is a 'dimmer' switch on your abilities of 1-10 (one being the lowest). I advise keeping a level of two or three, especially if you are in teens to early twenties, as information overloads will only fry your system.
  - If the above step is difficult, know that dreams are a nightly excursion where you can fly as much as you want, while

remaining grounded the following day. For more detailed exercises, go to the dream and forest chapters.

- Cover your head; wear a hat. This will keep the clairvoyant "dimmer" at a comfortable level, regardless of your ability to control it yourself.

## How to Notice the Messages of Departed Ones

*She slipped her prayers inside the book at the library of souls, to be taken to the ladder that connected both worlds and carried to the Throne by those that once lived and were yet to be born . . .*

Every prayer, tear, laugh, or action, is recorded and accounted for in a higher dimension. Having been between worlds, I can assure you that nothing is ever done in vain. Or ever truly lost.

Divine guidance comes a variety of ways: through dreams, words, books, people, or more. Therefore, it is important to be discerning and verify the origins of messages that appear to be coming through from the other side. Ask questions, explore whether or not the information aligns with your core values and faith. Does it come from that which is holy? Any nagging feelings of unease is your soul letting you know that, whatever it is, it is not right for your life. If you take honest inventory of where you are in the moment, without justifying or rationalizing, whether your path is authentic or dangerously off-track will quickly become obvious. I recommend daily prayer every morning, to set the tone and your regular intention to connect to Source. Let's face it: do you really think your dear loved ones need you to go to a stranger to communicate with your soul?

When our departed loved ones truly need to give us information, they will find a way. It can be in dreams or by directing our attention to things in our environment, such as specific codes or words that capture our focus. If you see consistent word or number patterns over the course of a couple days, or even weeks, this is a good indication that a loved one might be trying to draw your attention to something. This is only done to let you know they are ok, and not to make you paranoid.

These revelations make more sense if we first establish that death is only a matter of physical separation. The body and soul are no longer connected, but the soul lives on, no longer constrained by our space–time continuum. One of my teachers used to say; "One day to a soul in Heaven is a lifetime for us on Earth."

The more balanced you are in life—the calmer and more connected you are to your spiritual essence—the more you will be aware of hidden messages from the upper worlds. If you are swimming in negativity or highly reactive with your emotions, you will remain blind to the psychic senses. Center yourself. This will make it more possible for you to see and decipher the messages.

**Lost and Found**

*I placed my hands on the holy scroll for the first time and felt the fire of the letters penetrate the parchment to my soul. I sent a message of thanksgiving to the Merciful for restoring my life. That night I had a dream: in my hands I held a large white fruit that was soft inside. The texture turned into fine snow that I began to eat with a spoon. Each bite made me quiver and my soul began to vibrate; it was pure ecstasy. I found myself looking for my* siddur *(prayer book). The rabbi appeared and said that whatever I lost could be found again. His wife walked in holding the book in her hands; she had kept it safe.*

I woke up.

A few weeks later, the *siddur* I prayed with as a young child was returned after being lost for twenty-five years. My mother had found it hidden behind a drawer. The prayers I said as a child returned to find me as an adult.

A prayer that emanates from the soul is eternal.

## Thought as Prayer

There is a common Hasidic saying: *Think good, and it will be good.* If we could see what depression, anger, greed, and envy look like energetically (as compared to joy, focus, and gratitude), then we would be more careful in how they choose their thoughts. As I have described, I have seen slimy, sticky, wormlike energetic entities coming out of people when they doing things against the soul. I have seen dark forms energetically wrapped around adulators, and even entities that have hairs and threads to attach themselves to suck people's energy. As you start to understand the energetic nature of our relationships, recognize that you might be affecting others in a similar manner.

- Be mindful of you moods and the causes of them.
  - If you are moody, don't show it.

- Feed people. It is work to prepare the food, an act of compassion to offer it freely, and will guarantee that you will always have company.
- We must take time to give of ourselves to others. Keep in mind that there are many forms of giving. Sometimes, we must receive in order to allow someone else to give. In this way, both giving and receiving become G-dly actions.
- Observe the humble ant, one of the greatest builders in the universe. They can lift up to 5,000 times their own body weight, and they use this to their advantage. They spend their life working in their colony in synergy with the other ants to ensure the survival and continuance of their species. Nobody has to tell them what to do, nor can they afford to act out on a mood. As the wise King Solomon wrote, "Go to the ant, see her ways and grow wise. Though there is neither officer nor guard no ruler over her, she prepares her bread in summer and gathers her food in the Harvest time" (Proverbs 6; 6–7).

**A Rare Jewel**

How often do we hear a story of someone going through tragedy and becoming stronger—even greater—because of it? Many of us have come to expect the path of suffering as a means to learn our lessons. It is a natural, but unfortunate tendency that humans only delve into the deep waters of the soul when those things we hold dear are taken from us.

How can we stay inspired when we lose faith? Most of us are not there. We need to see the good revealed to us—or at least know it is in sight—to keep going. Change your mindset. While on this path, ask to be given the grace to know the events around us are unfolding as part of the Divine plan.

Some individuals operating at a high level of consciousness believe in greater good, even when utter tragedy befalls them. One of these individuals was a five-year-old boy named Raphael who had cancer. I remember once playing with him at his house. Though he had a feeding tube from his nostril down to his stomach, he was laughing and moving around, directing the adults on how to play Legos with him. Despite all that he had to endure, he chose to be joyful. We can learn such inspiring life lessons from this great teacher.

## Angel on Fire

One Friday night in 2001, I was a guest in the house of a friend from meditation school in Palos Verdes, close to L.A. There were five of us in the house, including her six-year-old son asleep in his bed. At approximately 11:30 at night, her boyfriend, a meditation instructor at the ashram where we all studied, decided to do an invocation to Archangel Michael as a prayer of protection before sleep. When he was finished, I noticed a bright being standing in the room, which became very hot. I could not tell if it was male or female; I sensed it was both. The hair and body were made of fire, the face hidden from the flames.

The angel led me to a closet in the hallway where the gas heater was located. When I saw it, I turned to the others and told them to open all the windows. Then,

I asked them to call the gas company and report a leak. My friend's boyfriend, the meditation instructor, felt it was unnecessary, as he had already said a prayer of protection. While this was true, I felt guided to take physical action as well.

Later, I learned that the mindset at the mediation school was in direct contrast to Jewish teachings, which don't nullify our responsibility to protect ourselves and take action when called for. The Supreme Being wants an active partner, not a passive one.

I insisted they call the gas company and open the windows immediately. As soon as the technician arrived, after about twenty minutes, the angel left. The technician inspected the heater, gasped, and shut it off. He said it was a textbook case of a carbon monoxide leak and a fire hazard: the flame from the furnace was jetting out towards the wooden door of the closet. If we had gone to sleep that night, we would have (G-d forbid) died from carbon monoxide poisoning or the house would have burned down with us inside.

The next day, we all attended the ashram for a "Healing and seeing Energy" workshop. Though the "master" knew lives were saved, it was not deemed as important as students to see an aura. Like so many other situations in the school, I questioned this. To me, the sanctity and value of a life is more important than esoteric, difficult-to-verify information. The priorities felt absurd and wrong.

Whether one believed I saw an angelic messenger or not, six lives were saved. I have not seen an angel on fire since, but I know they are around. Divine instruments sent from the Almighty are always acting as messengers and protectors on our behalf, without interfering in our free will.

## The Importance of Tithing

Everything we receive in this world—be it health, wealth, our families, homes, or work—is an opportunity. Our freedom to pursue our own endeavors is a privilege! With so much injustice in the world, how many innocent people are not at liberty to earn a living, due to tyranny and war? By sharing with others, we offer gratitude for the blessings we have.

It is an obligation to give a portion of what we receive back to G-d. Yet, how do we do this? What could the Creator possibly need from us? We have free will for a reason. It is to give us the ability to choose to do acts of kindness. To be compassionate and withhold judgment from those who appear to be suffering. We cannot fully know anyone else's story or the reason for their circumstances. I guarantee any success we currently enjoy comes from the cumulative efforts of many other people's intentions as well, both supporters and detractors, who help shape the experiences that have led us to this moment. If we only give when we feel like it, or if we only give selfishly—to make ourselves feel good—this is not true giving, true kindness. Since the world is sustained through compassion, it is not only spiritual, but also necessary for existence to give.

When I was five years old, or so my father tells, he gave me my first five-dollar bill. I put it in my pocket and we went for a walk down the streets of Chicago, where I saw a blind homeless man. I gave him my money and walked away. This kind of charity is not done for kudos. How could it be? I do not even remember the moment, but I like how this story illustrates how children will often naturally share what they have with those in need. Anyone who has been around kids will agree that they can be some of the most generous individuals. Conversely, teenagers can quickly become hardened and numb from real or imagined fears that have been conditioned into their psyches by their environments and constant exposure to media and other external controls. This can prevent them from doing acts of kindness. What a problem! Consider this. Our sages tell us: **It is said that for the world to continue there must be a minimum of thirty-six** *tzaddikim* (righteous individuals) **existing in the world at all times**. Hidden at times, these special souls uphold and keep the world in balance.

You are irreplaceable. No one else can touch the world with the same fingerprint as you. Each moment and every choice you make affects the future. Never underestimate how your actions will touch the next generations. Any person you ever assist in some way becomes your child, your friend, and everyone involved in the interaction, along with their descendants, may benefit. Though you might not know this consciously, your soul does and dances in the knowledge that you have just helped to tip the scale.

## Live from the Place of Love

Every day, try to be the best person you can be. When you fail, try again. Take time to notice and appreciate your surroundings. There is more beauty and love in the world then we can possibly imagine.

It is important not to judge the suffering of others based on their "karma." Certainly enough innocent people are martyred for their beliefs or skin color, whether from lack of soul awareness or moral compass in the face of evil.

Society has created certain ideas about which possessions and gifts make a person powerful, such as physical strength, money, position, or education. However, true power is not defined by external forces, but by qualities that reflect our soul. The path to achieving this starts within, by feeding and soothing the soul. Just as external forces do not define power, they also cannot be used to acquire power.

Throughout history, fear has been a popular tool employed by power-hungry individuals. It may work to a certain extent, but fear has its limitations. The most prevailing instrument of power is love. Love comes from within and knows no bounds; it must be felt in order to spread it to others. Want to feel real power? Open your heart and love someone. Want to become enlightened? Train the inner beast within to go with the flow and deal with life and humanity as a *mensch*!

I remember when I was in the meditation school, before our teacher the guru came to town, many of us would become hardcore about our bodies so that our auras would appear pure. We would abstain from meat, alcohol, our partners, or any place that was not considered spiritually elevated. If we went to a public place, we would bring our aura sprays, or silk, which was thought to protect against contamination from negative energies. It was a majorly obsessive-compulsive way to live, and about as spiritually prideful as one could get. I share this with you only to demonstrate how far down the wrong path one can go, even with the best of intentions.

This focus on constantly maintaining a positive aura began to skew my perception. One day I was in a restaurant and people began to resemble the faces of animals. I was seeing all kinds of things that were (a) none of my business and (b) coming from a very judgmental place. Shortly after, I moved to Seattle and away from all that. I spoke with my friend Rebbetzin Nechama and told her about the freaky day when people's faces morphed while eating pancakes. She suggested that I should train myself only to see the good in others and judge others favorably. Regardless of what I saw, it was only the outer layer of the aura, not necessarily the light from the soul within. She was absolutely right! (Besides, am I so perfect?) It was a revelation that has contributed to my greater happiness, and I try and use this advice in my dealings with others. This is not to say that your preference should be disregarded in favor of others with opposite tastes. We have free will to choose our lifestyle and whom we share it with. The lesson is not to take it personally when others choose something different. Opposing natures can work as long as the core values are similar. Most importantly, we are *all* a work in progress.

## Coming Home

In Judaism, when we speak of repentance, we use the word 'teshuva', whose literal translation, 'to return', connotes coming home to our Divine nature. Only then can we gather together and put our differences aside. Our intuitive nature is to be kind, joyful, to recognize freedom of choice. We access this nature and connect to our soul when we:

> *Live life with meaningful purpose*
> *Place the needs of a loved one above our desires.*
> *Befriend a lonely person.*

*Comfort the sick and bereaved.*
*Feel joy and give joy in whatever way we can.*
*Celebrate not only our own but the success of others.*

The essence of a good deed creates meaning in our daily actions, which makes us a partner with The Divine. Whatever your age, race, or religion, as long as you have breath in your body, your actions matter. Yet, we can find inspiration. Even in the darkest of times, a great Soul reveals unthinkable courage, faith, and even hope.

## "In spite of everything, I still believe that people are really good at heart."
### Anne Frank

Kabbalah teaches us that the Master of the World recreates this world every single second. HE decides what will be and what will not. We are here in this moment because we have a purpose. Our talents, our gifts, our energies, are all fundamental to the running of this world.
So go out and be a light amongst nations . . .
The world is waiting for you.

# ABOUT THE AUTHOR

*With over 20 years of experience, Tyger Kahn is a natural-born Clairvoyant and Clairaudient whose ancestry dates back to King David. She is a direct descendent of legendary healers, miracle workers, and prominent Kabbalists of Eastern Europe.*

*Kahn's unique and diversified background provides her with the life experience to recognize that we all have enormous potential. Tyger's international clientele include Fortune 500 executives, celebrities, healers, athletes, as well as medical and tech professionals.*

*Tyger has been featured in many popular magazines, including **W Magazine's "Black Book"** & **LA Magazine's "Best of LA"**. She has also been featured on numerous radio shows worldwide, such as **Hay House Radio** and **Wake Up Tucson**. She has served as an advisor for eight years for **Tibetan Healing Fund**, Tibet's first freestanding birth center, which opened its doors in the town of Repkong in 2009. She has taught workshops on developing intuition for **Chabad** in the Pacific Northwest and **the New Synagogue in Palm Beach**. Tyger Kahn is currently teaching mindfulness and intuitive workshops in Seattle.*

## The Kabbalistic Artist

The cover of this book came about indirectly from people who broke my heart in a tremendously challenging time in my life. Alone, without family or friends in my new hometown, I had just recovered from my ordeal with cancer. I felt so isolated and scared, I retreated to my true places of comfort: the woods and the synagogue. At the latter, I shared stories of the forest and its magic, volunteering in the children's program. One day, in the midst of a terrific tale, I glanced at a painting that hung on the wall and my soul began to dance. The artist had captured a glimpse of Shamayim. Over the next several years, the light returned to me, and I wrote and wrote and wrote. Through a series of incredible events, the same mystical artist made the cover for this book.

## My Lineage

For those who would like to know more about my lineage, continue reading.

My father is a Holocaust survivor from Transylvania who had his children late in life. (The stories of his life alone could fill a book.) My Canadian mother was much younger than he when they married. They are profoundly different from one another with one exception: they are each directly descended from giant players in Jewish history. These are people whose premonitions saved towns and entire communities—who gave blessings that were fulfilled. Their abilities were passed down throughout the ages to their descendants. I happen to be one of the recipients.

When I was nine, I used to sneak into my father's library to read his books on Kabbalah. There were so many! But he quickly stopped my efforts. He came from a school of thought where, unless you were forty, married, male, and had already studied the Torah for decades, the Book of Splendor was forbidden. There were many reasons for this: Without proper preparation, the energy emanating from the Holy Zohar (the book of

Kabbalah) is dangerous. One could lose one's mind, or worse, upon reading. It is certainly not reading material for a nine-year-old girl! It is not like I understood much of what I read, though sometimes I would run my hands over the Hebrew letters and they later would appear in my dreams as black fire in a white space. (Dad soon figured this out and hid the books.)

As you now know, I have had wild dreams my whole life. When I was younger, my father sometimes interpreted them. He would listen carefully to my nocturnal visions, then proclaim in a rolling Transylvanian accent, *"Mar'eh Yechskal Einacle!"* In English, this means "a daughter of the Master Yecheskal"—Ezekial Paneth, my great-great-grandfather (whom I refer to affectionately as my *zeyde*), the Chief Rabbi of Transylvania. He is also my favorite ancestor and the one to whom I feel closest. Ezekial Paneth was a great Kabbalistic mystic and author of eighteen books. Because of his unique gifts, he was given broad powers by the government.

In one famous incident, my zeyde had a vision that a Turkish army would invade his ancient Romanian town. Before they arrived, he ushered the entire community (Jews and non-Jews) into his synagogue where, he told them, they would be protected. As zeyde predicted, the synagogue was attacked. To this day you can see cannonballs lodged in the walls. But again, as my zeyde foretold, the people were unharmed. In gratitude for what they considered a miracle, the Austro-Hungarian government gave my zeyde a black-and-gold chariot to ride in and a personal seal with a Latin inscription that translates roughly to "super-rabbi."

Of the stories of his life (which can be read in Hebrew in the biography *Mar'eh Yechskal ha-Shalem,* by Ezekiel Paneth (2 Vols.), many demonstrate how much he cared for women and children. The next story is no exception: There was a man from Poland who, after abandoning his wife and family to fend for themselves, arrived in Carlsberg, where my zeyde's synagogue was located. It was in the mountains and a good place to hide—or so the man thought. After finding out the reason behind the man's journey, my zeyde had him arrested and threw him in the jail of the synagogue. Zeyde would not release him until the man signed a *get* (document for a Jewish divorce) for his wife. That way, the woman could be freed from her unsupportive husband and remarry. Without the get, she would be chained to her marriage. Subsequently, my zeyde issued an edict to further protect women from penniless abandonment. Every new man joining the town had to be sketched, and these documents were to be used in case the person tried to flee his family. Zeyde helped over three hundred women—and this was before the Internet! The Romanian government put up a shrine in his honor. To this day, people gather to pray at his gravesite, believing that *tzaddikim*, like my zeyde, leave a portion of the soul's imprint in their bones.

In addition to interpreting my dreams, my father would tell me stories, often about my relatives. Once such story took place when my father was 5. His grandfather, who was 105 years old at that point, asked for relatives to visit on the Friday before Sabbath. This was a strange request, as the time was drawing near to prepare for Shabbat. Since he was considered a *tzaddik,* they obliged. My father remembers standing in his grandfather's room, packed with people. He watched his zeyde bless each descendant, then take his *tallit* (Jewish prayer shawl), wrap it around his body, say good-bye, close his eyes, and die.

It is very inspiring to hear stories of individuals going to meet the Creator with such courage and clarity. From this, we know my zeyde was a highly realized soul. Even before death, he was filled with compassion for others and gave each person in the room a blessing. Portraying unconditional love and perfect faith are two of my zeyde's characteristics that I aspire to emulate.

### The Priestly Family: Kahana
The stories of my ancestors are too numerous to write here, but here is some of my background for those who are interested.

The Kahana family is descended from the daughters of the Talmudic commentator and scholar, Rashi, whose commentaries on the books of Moses, Writings, and Prophets are widely regarded as fundamental to Jewish study and life. Rashi is a descendant of King David. On my father's side, tradition says the Kahana family is one of the ancient families left from the tribe of Judah.

Named the Tapuchim (in English, Apples), they were taken as war trophies by Roman Emperor, Titus, and paraded through the streets of Rome in the year 71.

The relationship between the Apple and Kahana family goes through Rabbi Moshe HaLevi Wallerstein, Ashkenazi Chief Rabbi of the sixteenth century. His grandson, Rabbi Gershon Shaul Yom-Tov Lipman Heller Wallerstein HaLevi (1579–1654), is my direct ancestral zeyde on my father's side.

Rabbi Yom-Tov Lipman Heller, also known as Tosafot Yom-Tov, was a giant Talmudic sage and Kabbalist in Prague in the 17<sup>th</sup> century, who later went on to become chief Rabbi of the *Beit Din* (Jewish Court) in many cities, including Austria, Prague, and Krakow. He is best known for writing a commentary on the Oral Torah called the *Tosafot Yom-Tov*. Currently, his portrait hangs in the Kunsthistorisches Museum in Vienna, entitled *Man at the Window* (1653) by Samuel Van Hoogstraten 1627–78. His works are still being published today; including his autobiography that was later completed and published by his son, entitled *A Chronicle of Hardship and Hope*. To this day, I hold copies of this work, which speaks of his life, miracles, adversity and redemption, and hope for the future. Although he suffered such hardships and betrayals, he continued to keep his faith and to inspire others. It is humbling to be his descendent and to read his words, which lend guidance to even today's challenges. I highly recommend reading his autobiography and also his personal story, which can be found in the book *The Feast and the Fast*.

## About the Baal Shem Tov (1698-1760)

I am also descended from Rabbi Yisroel ben Eliezer, also known as the Baal Shem Tov; a miracle worker, healer, founder of Hassidic Judaism, and considered one of the greatest mystics Judaism has ever known. He was one of the thirty-six hidden tzaddikim who incarnate in every generation to ensure the world does not collapse from evil. His message is of serving the Creator with joy and brotherly love.

The Baal Shem Tov has been well documented as a miracle worker in cases where he cured the sick, healed the broken-hearted, and communicated with animals, nature, and even hidden realms. Information about the Baal Shem Tov, which means 'Master of the Good Name', is so vast, it would fill a library. Many of his parables serve as excellent tools to study the ways of compassion, truth, and higher knowledge.

## GLOSSARY

**Ani Ma'amin** — Hebrew; translates as 'I believe redemption will come'.

**Anne Frank** — German Jew of the 20<sup>th</sup> Century; widely known for her diary on her life, detailing her time spent hiding from the Nazis during World War II before she was taken to the concentration camps; she is one of the most well-known Holocaust victims.

**Aura** — translucent sheath that encapsulates the gross material dimensions of the body and contains the light emanating from the soul.

**Baal Shem Tov (Rabbi Yisroel ben Eliezer)** — Hebrew, meaning 'Master of a Good Name'; Mystical Rabbi in 18<sup>th</sup> Century Ukraine; founder of Chasidic Judaism.

**Bechira** — Hebrew for 'choice'; denotes free will.

**Beit Din** — Hebrew for 'house of judgment'; Jewish Court.

**Beshert** — Yiddish, meaning 'soul mate'.

**Bimah** — Hebrew, meaning 'alter' or 'podium'; usually refers to where the Torah is read from in a Synagogue and from where the service is led.

**Challah** — Hebrew; Braided bread baked specifically for Shabbat.

**Chatzitza** — Hebrew, meaning 'barrier'.

**Chessed** — Hebrew; Random acts of kindness and

goodness; one of the three pillars of the world, according to Kabbalah.

**Chutzpah** — Yiddish, meaning 'full of audacity' or 'impertinence'; used today as slang.

**Clairaudient** — A more rare form of clairvoyance in which information pertaining to reality is picked up via the sense of sound.

**Clairvoyant** — An individual with the ability to perceive future events or that, which is beyond ordinary sensory contact.

**Cohen** (plural, **Cohanim**) — Hebrew; A Jewish priest.

**Emet** — Hebrew meaning 'truth'; refers to Divine, G-dly truth.

**Emunah** — Hebrew for 'belief'; means innate conviction that transcends reason.

**Energy Centers** (also known as **chakras**) — Concentrated swirling balls of light that make up an aura.

**Ezer Kenegdo** — Hebrew, meaning 'a helpmate in opposition to, next to, or against'; refers to the relationship of woman to men.

**Gilgul** — Hebrew; means 'wheel' or 'cycle'; refers to reincarnation.

**Hannah Szenes** — 1921-1944; Israeli heroine; Paratrooper, sent to rescue Hungarian Jews in Yugoslavia from the Nazi death camps; was captured, tortured, and killed by the Nazis without releasing the details of her mission; widely known for her poetry.

**Havdallah** — Hebrew, meaning 'separation'; ceremony at the end of Shabbat; meant to illuminate the light of the Sabbath for rest of the week.

**Hitbodedut** — Hebrew; translates as self-seclusion; refers to an unstructured form of meditation and prayer, meant to establish a personal relationship with the Almighty and gain a better understanding of oneself; a main teaching of Rabbi Nachman of Breslov.

**Kabbalah** — Hebrew for 'receive'; Jewish mysticism.

**Ketubah** — Hebrew; Marriage contract in Jewish weddings.

**Kiddush** — Hebrew for 'holy' or 'sanctified'; ceremony of blessings made over wine. Typically made by head of Jewish household (male) to bring in the Sabbath, or on other holy days.

**Mensch** — Yiddish; an upright individual, known to have honor and/or integrity.

**Mezuzah** (plural, **mezuzot**) — Hebrew; a parchment inscribed with paragraphs of the Jewish prayer, Shema; is attached to doorposts in a Jewish house (typically seen on the front doorpost) as a sign of faith.

**Mikveh** — Hebrew for "collection of water"; a body of water in which certain Jewish rituals regarding purification are preformed.

**Mitzvah** (plural, **mitzvot**) — Hebrew; translates as a 'commandment'; an instruction that allows for connection to the Divine.

**Modeh Ani** — Hebrew; literally means, "I am admitting/thanking"; this is the ancient Jewish prayer typically to be said in the morning after waking, thanking the Creator for returning the soul back to the body.

**Nefesh** — Hebrew; Animal soul; male; instinctive; connected to the physical world.

**Ner Tamid** — Hebrew for "everlasting light"; refers to a lamp above the ark in a Synagogue that is kept constantly burning to symbolize G-d's eternal presence in our lives.

**Neshama** — Hebrew; The feminine aspect of a being's soul.

**Prophet** (as opposed to **seer**) — A person who proclaims the will of god; prophets are seers, but seers are not necessarily prophets. The term 'seer' refers to a lower level of prophecy.

**Rabbi Nachman of Breslov** — Highly influential Rabbi of the late 18th Century; founder of Breslov Chasidic movement; the great-grandson of the Baal Shem Tov.

**Rachamim** — Hebrew; denotes mercy.

**Rebbetzin** — Yiddish; A Jewish female teacher of knowledge; the wife of a Rabbi.

**Ribbono Shel Olam** — Hebrew for 'Master of the Universe'; one of the names of G-d.

**Rosh Chodesh** — Hebrew; means 'head of the month'; denotes the first day/s of a new month in the Hebrew calendar.

**Ruach** — Hebrew for 'air', 'breath', 'wind', 'spirit'. Also refers to a level of the Divine soul.

**Seer** (as opposed to **prophet**) — Individual who can see into the future via supernatural forces,

**Shabbat** (also referred to as) — Hebrew; means to 'sit' or 'dwell'; Jewish day of rest from creation/creating, held from sundown Friday until sundown Saturday.

**The Sabbath** — Day of rest; held on Friday, Saturday, or Sunday depending on your identification.

**Shamayim** — Hebrew; meaning 'Heaven' or 'sky'.

**Shekinah** — Hebrew; The feminine aspect of G-d.

**Shema** — Hebrew; means 'hear'; Ancient prayer that declares the oneness and greatness of G-d; parts of this prayer are used it the mezuzah.

**Shemittah** — Hebrew; Ritual of resting the land in Israel every seventh year.

**Shidduch** — Hebrew, originally Aramaic; Jewish matchmaking for the purpose of marriage.

**Shofar** — Hebrew; An ancient wind instrument fashioned from a ram's horn, originally used in Jewish ceremonies as a sign for battle; blown on Rosh Hashanah and Yom Kippur.

**Siddur** — Hebrew; Jewish prayer book.

**Sir Arthur Conan Doyle** — British physical and writer, most notable for his series about detective, Shirlock Holmes.

**Song of Songs** — A book written by King Solomon, where the ultimate relationship between man and G-d is symbolized through the relationship between a husband and wife.

**Tallit** — Hebrew; Jewish prayer shawl with four fringed corners known as tzitzit.

**Tefilat HaDerech** — Hebrew; called the wayfarer's prayer in English; typically said at the beginning of any journey, as it is thought to evoke Divine mercy and bring safe travels.

**Tefillin** — Hebrew for 'phylacteries'; Two small black boxes containing specific prayers connected to two black straps made of leather; worn on forehead and left forearm of Jewish men during Morning Prayer; reminder to keep the commandments of Jewish law.

**Tehillim** — Hebrew; Book of Psalms, mainly written by King David; typically sung or recited both formally and informally as part of Jewish prayer.

**Teshuva** — Hebrew; literal translation means, 'to return'; repentance.

**Tikkun** — Hebrew; meaning 'correction' and 'repair'.

**Tuchas** — Yiddish word for 'butt'; origin of the English word, 'tush'.

**Tzaddik** (plural **tzaddikim**) — Hebrew; colloquially refers to a righteous individual; the term also refers to holy men that can act as a pipeline, of sorts, between man and G-d.

**Zechut** — Hebrew for 'merit'

**Zeyde** — Yiddish for 'grandfather'; I use it affectionately to refer to my great-great-grandfather, Ezekial
Paneth.